PLANNING AND DESIGNING EFFECTIVE METRICS

Martin Klubeck

Apress®

Planning and Designing Effective Metrics

ISBN-13 (pbk): 978-1-4842-0827-4

ISBN-13 (electronic): 978-1-4842-0826-7

Managing Director: Welmoed Spahr
Lead Editor: Jeff Olson
Technical Reviewer: Russ Cheesman
Editorial Board: Steve Anglin, Mark Beckner, Gary Cornell, Louise Corrigan, James DeWolf,
    Jonathan Gennick, Robert Hutchinson, Michelle Lowman, James Markham,
    Matthew Moodie, Jeff Olson, Jeffrey Pepper, Douglas Pundick, Ben Renow-Clarke,
    Gwenan Spearing, Matt Wade, Steve Weiss
Coordinating Editor: Annie Beck, Rita Fernando
Copy Editor: Kimberly Burton
Compositor: Mary Sudul
Indexer: SPi Global
Artists: Martin Klubeck and Alyssa Klubeck
Cover Designer: Anna Ishchenko

Distributed to the book trade worldwide by Springer Science+Business Media New York, 233 Spring Street, 6th Floor, New York, NY 10013. Phone 1-800-SPRINGER, fax (201) 348-4505, e-mail orders-ny@springer-sbm.com, or visit www.springeronline.com.

For information on translations, please e-mail rights@apress.com, or visit www.apress.com.

Apress and friends of ED books may be purchased in bulk for academic, corporate, or promotional use. eBook versions and licenses are also available for most titles. For more information, reference our Special Bulk Sales–eBook Licensing web page at www.apress.com/bulk-sales.

For my children and my wife. My best measures of success are your levels of happiness.

Contents

About the Author

Martin Klubeck is a strategy and planning consultant at the University of Notre Dame and a recognized expert in the field of practical metrics. He holds a master's degree from Webster University in human resources development and a bachelor's in computer science from Chapman University. Other books by Martin include; *Why Organizations Struggle So Hard to Improve So Little, Metrics: How to Improve Key Business Results*, and *The Professional Development Toolbox*. His passion for simplifying the complex has led to the development of a simple system for developing meaningful metrics. Klubeck is also the founder of the Consortium for the Establishment of Information Technology Performance Standards, a nonprofit organization focused on providing much-needed standards for measures. You can find more information about Martin and his efforts in simplifying the complex at his website, MKKnowledgeBuilders.com.

About the Technical Reviewer

Russ Cheesman is a senior information technology professional and consultant with experiences in all phases of the System Development Life Cycle. Much of his career had been devoted to enabling IT solutions for business problems and/or opportunities. He has served as an IT manager and practitioner in many industry sectors, including banking/financial, manufacturing, construction, retail, pharmaceutical, telecommunications, and health care. Mr. Cheesman, in recent years, has been practicing business performance measurement and management within several IT and health care organizations through the use of business strategy, balanced scorecards, metrics, key performance indicators, and business analytical systems.

Mr. Cheesman was happy to serve as the senior technical reviewer for this book and related concepts on metrics, and looks forward to its release and subsequent value to all those individuals, groups, and organizations that desire improvement, continuous maturation, and peak performance.

Acknowledgments

The purpose of an acknowledgment, as I understand it, is to let those people who helped make this achievement possible know that I didn't forget their contributions. This chore makes this easily the most stressful part of writing a book.

I don't want to forget any of my friends or colleagues who helped me by reviewing, critiquing, or suggesting edits to the work as it was in progress, especially: Don Padgett, Danita Leese, Leah Lang, Keith (Mac) McIntosh, Marin Stanek, and my brother Irving. Thanks for the short-notice reads. Thanks for the kind words. And thanks for being there.

Of course, Russ Cheesman has to be thanked for his work as my technical reviewer. Although Russ and I disagreed as often as we agreed about metrics and their use, when asked for a recommendation, I immediately thought of Russ for the job. His honest and passionate position, his large knowledge base, and his expertise made him an easy choice. Thanks, Russ, for your hard work, your many suggestions, and your honest appraisals.

I want to give a special thanks to Michael Langthorne. Not only were you my most dependable reviewer, but your early and consistent encouragement to take this journey, on my own, was instrumental to me starting and finishing this work. I appreciate your help, guidance, and gentle but steady shoves very much. Thanks. I truly could not have done this without you.

I also want to thank Jeff Olson, Kimberly Burton, and Annie Beck. Although you made up the Apress editorial team, and were "just doing your jobs," I can't say I saw you that way. I greatly appreciate your help. You were honest, consistent, and fair. You were focused on producing the best product possible for Apress while showing sincere concern for my position as an author. Someday, if the chance ever arrives, I'm buying the first round.

Last, but as the saying goes, not least, I want to thank my family. Especially my wife, Kristine. This time around, you successfully feigned interest in my progress, if not in the work itself. I appreciate the effort and I love you dearly. Alyssa, thanks for your help with the fairy tales and allowing me to use your art work for the book. I look forward to seeing your name on more jacket covers. I love you.

And a final, special thank you to you, whoever you are, reading this book. You are special—you must be because no one reads the acknowledgements unless they think they'll find their name listed. So you must be one of the rare people who read books from cover to cover. That means you may also be the type of reader who will use the material within these pages. You may also be the type of person who will share your thoughts, likes, and dislikes. So, here's to hoping I hear from you and thanks in advance for any feedback you choose to share. I hope this book helps you navigate the sometimes dangerous waters of developing metrics.

Note 1 This book is an abridged version of my book, *Metrics: How To Improve Key Business Results* (Apress, 2011). We thought a shorter version of the book might help those who have a more focused need on just getting a metrics program started. This version is intended to provide the minimum needed to be successful in creating meaningful metrics.

Since this abridged version of *Metrics: How To Improve Key Business Results* is a child of the original, the acknowledgments are the same except I'd like to offer another thanks to the Apress team for believing enough in my mission of simplifying metrics that they championed this version.

Note 2 While I have worked hard to provide you, the reader, with real examples (real situations, interactions, experiences, measures, and data), I had to temper that effort with protecting the privacy and data owned by others. To this end, I have, where necessary, blended and combined individuals into composites. I have also done the same with data. As you will read, I fully believe that data is "owned" by the provider(s) of that data, so I have protected the identities and data of those whose experiences I used for much of this book.

Metrics: The Basics

An Introduction

Of all the possible organizational-improvement tools, metrics stands out for me as the most requested, misunderstood, feared—and useful. Defining metrics from a high level requires that I give you the What, Why, When, Where, Who, and How.

What

For me, metrics are a means of telling a complete story for the purpose of improving something. Usually, the idea is to improve an organization. Sometimes, though, you will want to focus on improving a process. In the end, anything you improve should align back to improvements that help the organization.

Metrics are a tool for improvement. By their nature, metrics use different levels of information to tell a story. Although I always strive to make this story comprehensive, it's nearly impossible to capture everything. In most cases, I try to capture enough of what's important to help with the improvement.

Metrics affect the improvement effort by helping you determine what was wrong in the first place, how well your efforts have worked (did you improve and did you improve as much as you wanted?), and what the new environment looks like after the change. I say "change" because improvement requires change. It doesn't have to be drastic. It could mean that you do something new, you stop doing something, or you do something differently. But, improvement doesn't come about without some change.

Albert Einstein said, "The definition of insanity is doing the same things, the same way, and expecting a different result."

The following are just a few of the things a metrics program can help you do:

- Improve company "health" in a variety of areasImprove customer satisfaction
    - Improve product/service value
    - Improve employee satisfaction
    - Improve process efficiency
    - Improve strategy, planning, and execution
- Provide a basis for change
    - What to change
    - When to change
    - How to change
- Lay a foundation for understanding your organization by providing insights into
    - strengths
    - problems
    - weaknesses
    - opportunities

Metrics are about change for the purpose of improvement. At least that's how I use them. I'm an idealist, and you'll see that reflected in my belief that metrics can be a powerful tool for improvement.

Why

Why metrics? To improve. I know I've already stated that. But, why metrics specifically? Why not use any of the other methods du jour (TQM, Six Sigma, Balanced Scorecard, etc.)? The funny thing is, any of the methods you choose will require you to use metrics—or at least the components of metrics. As a foundation, these improvement methods want you to create a baseline to see how well the improvement effort worked. All of these methods also want you to measure the amount of time, money, and effort that went into the improvement. But none of that will actually help you improve the thing you want to improve!

Metrics will provide insights into the thing you want to improve—be it a product, service, or process. This insight is valuable to those doing the job—fulfilling the need or providing the service. It helps them see their efforts in a new light, often as a more complete picture. It will help them find ways to improve. It will also help them see the benefits they've reaped. It will provide cherished feedback that the team can use to make continuous improvement a reality (instead of the latest catch-phrase).

Metrics also provides insights for upper management. It allows the team leader to market the improvement effort to those who control the funding. It shines a light on his efforts so he can gain support for the improvement efforts.

It also allows you to share your efforts with your customers in ways they easily understand. They gain insight to how things are changing for the better. Look at any new product release (I especially like Apple's semi-annual announcements) and notice the amount of metrics sprinkled throughout.

Metrics provide insight. They also provide a level of legitimacy to your argument. All other things being equal, data is a tie breaker. If you and another department have competing requests for resources, the one with data wins.

When

Ideally, you'd not undertake a metrics effort of any significant scale until your organization could show that it was not suffering from organizational immaturity—the inability to take on enterprise-wide change. But, that's only a prerequisite for implementing a program organization-wide. If you are in charge of a department or unit and you want to implement a department-wide metrics program, you only have to ensure that your unit is capable of the change.

Chances are very good that you already collect data and measures. You may have automated tools that track, collect, and even spit out reports full of data and measures. You may feed information into an annual report. You may already fulfill requests for specific measures. Depending on your industry, there may be well-worn standards that have been used for years (if not decades). These are not necessarily metrics per my definition, nor are creating such standards the intent of this book. Those data and measures are reported, but not used. They aren't used to improve a process, product, or service.

It may be time for you to start using your information for your own benefit. It may be time for you to develop a metrics program. The major question you have to ask is, are you ready, willing, and able to change? Do you want to improve?

You'll learn in this book that part of the "when" is collecting information on the thing you want to improve *before* you attempt to make it better—just as good researchers do. So, the when is before you start, during, and after your improvement efforts.

Where

The metrics program should reside with the owner of the data. I spend 80 percent of my workday developing metrics for others. I coach my customers through the design, creation, implementation, and maintenance of the metrics. In many cases, I also produce and publish their metrics. But I happily tell anyone who asks that I don't own any of them. I am just helping the owners produce them. They are not mine. My greatest successes are when I can transfer the maintenance and publishing of the metrics to someone on the team who owns the metric. I then transition to a consultant role, helping them use and improve the metrics. This transition takes time—normally because of either a lack of skill or resources. But having the owner of the metric take over the production, maintenance, and publishing of them is always the ultimate goal for me.

So the metrics need to eventually reside in the data owner's domain. That can be on their office walls. It can be on their shared computer drive. It can be on their web site. That's where it belongs. But metrics show up in other places like annual reports, monthly meetings, and public web sites.

The publication of metrics will be up to the owner. The decision of where it will be published should be a careful decision based on the use of the metrics and the need for others to have access to the information. The more mature the organization, the more comfortable it will be with sharing the metrics. Many organizations are not mature enough to share metrics with their peers, their customers, and definitely not the public.

Who

I fulfill part of the "who" question on a daily basis. I am the producer of many of the metrics my organization uses. I am also the lead designer, collector, analyst, and publisher. But as stated in the Where section, I am always looking to transfer as much of this as possible to the metrics owner.

Who are the owners? The owners of the metrics are primarily those who are delivering the product, service, or carrying out the process. But ownership can be spread across the entire organization, depending on how you define the item being measured.

The key here isn't so much who owns the metric but in who doesn't. Don't exclude the frontline worker. Don't think the metric belongs to the CEO or upper management. If the metric is reported at those lofty heights, it doesn't mean they should reside only there. Remember the purpose of metrics. Unless the CEO and top managers are the ones improving the processes (and they rarely directly deliver products or services), then you have to include the people carrying out the work—the ones that will be responsible for making the improvements actual work. How much harm can be done if upper management finds out that a department was using metrics for improvement but hadn't shared them upstream? Some. But now imagine how much trouble can arise if a department finds out that upper management had been reviewing metrics about their processes, services, or products and they didn't even know. Will that significantly harm the organization? I'm willing to bet it will.

If upper management wants metrics on a department, unit, process, service, or product, all of those involved should be included in the distribution of those metrics. They should also be involved in the design, creation, and publication of them.

The simple answer to "who?" is this: everyone in the organization, with the frontline workers being the primary "who."

How

I offer you a comprehensive set of guidelines for developing metrics for improvement. I call them guidelines because "rules" would mean that I'm offering the only right way. As with most things, there's more than one right way to develop metrics. The language, processes, and tools I offer are a result of more than twenty years of experience. That experience was full of successes and failures. I learned from both and am happy to share the results so you won't have to fall into the same holes I did. And if you're already in one of those holes, my advice is simple: stop digging and climb out.

What You'll Find Inside

Having a common language for metrics and its components is an essential foundation for the conversation we'll engage in throughout this book. While putting this book together, and while thinking about all of the tools you can use to make your analysis and publishing of metrics easier, it struck me that there is another important distinction between metrics and other tools for improvement.

First and foremost, for me, metrics are in and of themselves tools for improvement. Even when using metrics to keep track of progress or predict future trends, metrics should be seen as a means for improvement. But that's not enough to distinguish it from a mass of other tools out there. I've used many tools to solve organizational problems. Total Quality Management, the Capability Maturity Model, Lean, and Lean Six Sigma are a few. Each of these improvement methodologies also uses data and measures. Six Sigma uses data throughout its processes, not only to measure improvement but to determine what to improve. There are also measures of success and goal attainment. There are even measures which turn ordinary wishes into SMART (specific, measurable, attainable, realistic, and time-bound) goals.

Many of the tools designed around metrics are for statistical analysis. These powerful tools can be used to determine relationships between different data, causal relationships, and even determine the accuracy of data.

But "metrics," for me, are much more and in some ways a bit less than a statistical analysis tool.

Metrics are not a statistician's dream or an analyst's favorite tool. The school of statistical analysis is much larger and deeper than I plan on digging. A common disclaimer I offer when teaching on metrics is that I am not a statistician, nor will the course include statistics. In these ways, metrics are a bit less.

But metrics are in many ways much more than statistics. They are a means of telling stories, and of providing valuable insights. Metrics are a tool for pointing out the correct direction to take when at a cross-roads—a choice between one improvement effort and another.

Metrics, for me, are the cornerstone of an organizational development program and a tool for answering the most important organizational questions.

It is these minor distinctions between metrics and other measurement-based tools for improvement that make this book a necessity. There are courses on statistics (one of my colleagues came to metrics by way of being a statistician), books on various analytical tools, and software tools developed for this purpose (SPSS, MiniTab, and Sigma XL, to name three). But there is little written or taught about the use of metrics. This deficiency has been partially addressed by Kaplan and Norton with their Balanced Scorecard methodology and by Dr. Dean Spitzer's book *Transforming Performance Measurement* (AMACOM, 2007). I intend to take their efforts to their logical and necessary next step—making the design, creation, and use of metrics practical for anyone.

Metrics will make it possible for you to use data, measures, and information to improve your organization and lead to the key business results you need to be a success.

I hope this book helps you to develop metrics that in turn help you improve your organization. Regardless of the size or mission of your organization, metrics can be a powerful tool for improvement, and this book will make metrics as simple as possible.

Establishing A Common Language

Data, and Measures, and Information, OH MY!

It is important to establish a simple, easy-to-understand language so that everyone, regardless of their experience or education, can understand the benefits metrics can provide. I believe a lack of a common language causes more problems in business (and life) than anything else. Developing a shared vocabulary is the first step in ensuring success.

I intend to use very common words, plain English as it were, to help make what seems complex into something very simple and straightforward.

Let's start with a story to get in the proper frame of mind.

The Three Little Pigs Go Large

There I was, trying to remember a fairy tale so I could get my three-year-old to sleep. She demanded a story, but being on the road without any of her books meant I had to remember one. Well, I have a terrible memory for stories—but an unfailing memory for lessons I've taught. So, like any good father, I improvised. What better way to get her to fall asleep than to tell a story about metrics?

The Story

After effectively dealing with their landlord (Mr. Wolf), the three little pigs settled into a life of luxury and over-indulgence. Three years passed, finding the pigs each living in squalor, dangerously overweight (even for a pig), and in failing health. Each visited his respective doctor. Each doctor came to the same prognosis: this pig was on the fast track to an early barbecue. The pigs did not eat well, sleep enough, exercise, nor did they pay attention to the signs their bodies were giving them. The doctors knew the pigs must change their lifestyles or they would die.

The First Little Pig

Unfortunately for the pigs, the doctors were also very much different. The first little pig's doctor told him that his health was failing and that he would have to change his lifestyle. The little pig needed to get serious about his health. The doctor sent the little pig away with a diet plan, an exercise plan, and an appointment to return in 12 months.

The first little pig was dutifully scared by his doctor's warnings, so he worked hard to change. He stopped eating unhealthy foods. He exercised daily. He even started going to sleep early. After one month, the first little pig felt great. He hadn't felt this good in years! He decided to celebrate. He went out with the lamb twins and partied all night. He had a feast that was followed by an ice cream eating contest (which he won). At about 3 AM he made it home and fell asleep, content on his bed. The next day he forgot to exercise. It was easy to get out of the habit. Eventually, he only exercised on weekends, reasoning that he was too busy during the week. By the end of the next month he was eating poorly again—not as badly as before—but not as good as he should have.

At the end of the year, when the first little pig returned to the doctor, he was shocked to hear that the doctor was disappointed.

> "But Doc, I did what you said," the first little pig pleaded. "I exercise and I eat better. I even go to sleep earlier. I know I'm healthier ... I feel better than I did last year."

> "Yes, but your weight did not improve enough. You may be eating better, but not well enough. You may be sleeping more, but still not enough. Your health is deteriorating overall ... and I fear that you are going to die if you don't change your ways."

The doctor gave the first little pig a new diet and exercise program. He even signed the first little pig up for a spinning class and prescribed medication. The doctor gave the little pig another appointment for the following year and wished him well. The first little pig was dutifully frightened by all of this and swore by his chinny chin chin (which was pretty large) that he'd do better.

This time the first little pig stayed on course. He exercised regularly and ate only healthy foods. When he was hungry he ate carrots, or celery, or non-fat yogurt. He attended the spinning classes every week, like clockwork. Unfortunately, with no way to measure his progress, the first little pig didn't know how well he was doing. After seven months, he felt better, but his anxiety about his health created so much stress that he had a stroke. While he had improved his health, he had not improved it enough to weather the physical needs a stroke put on his system. He died a month later. The first little pig's doctor was sad to learn of his death. He shed a tear as he removed the upcoming appointment from the calendar.

The Second Little Pig

The second little pig's doctor understood the importance of metrics. He was a good doctor who communicated well with his patients. He felt like a father to his patients and sought to help them become healthier. When the doctor looked over the second little pig's charts, he was dismayed. How to help the little pig change course? How could he help him get healthy? He liked metrics and thought the little pig would do well if he had some goals. The doctor designed a plan with three measures: weight, blood pressure, and cholesterol levels. He explained to the little pig that he was at risk for serious health problems. He told the little pig to lower his weight by 100 pounds, get his blood pressure down to recommended levels, and reduce the bad cholesterol levels to acceptable standards. He even gave the little pig a chart to track the three measures. When the little pig asked him for advice on how to achieve these goals, the doctor offered the little pig six pamphlets, two books, and a list of web sites that he could go to for identifying programs for getting healthy. The doctor scheduled follow up appointments every three months for the next year.

The second little pig worked very hard on his program. He posted the chart on his refrigerator. He changed his eating habits, started an exercise program, and tried meditation. He bought a blood pressure monitor, a high-quality scale, and a nifty kit for checking cholesterol levels. He didn't mind the expense—his health was worth it. He measured his blood pressure, weight, and cholesterol when he woke up—and twice more during the day. At his first quarterly checkup, the doctor was happy with his progress. They went over the numbers and decided the second little pig was on the right track. The pig was elated. He decided to step it up a bit. He thought about gastric bypass surgery, but opted instead for eating tofu six days a week. The seventh day, he would eat mixed vegetables. He stepped up his exercise program. He started on a cholesterol-lowering drug he learned about from his spam e-mail. (He loved spam.)

The second little pig's behaviors became more reckless as he neared his second checkup. He went on a water diet three days before and spent the morning of his appointment in a steam bath to shed the water weight. His doctor was amazed. The pig had lost a total of 60 pounds, improved his blood pressure, and lowered his cholesterol levels to within 10 percent of recommended levels. The doctor applauded his efforts and predicted success by his next appointment, three months hence.

Two months later the second little pig's kidneys failed and he died. The pig hadn't understood the overall goal or how to measure his overall health. He had spent the last eight months chasing a small set of numbers instead of developing "good health." He managed to improve his three areas of measurement, but neglected other areas of his health to do so.

The Third Little Pig

The third little pig's doctor also believed in metrics. He was also good with his patients, but he was different than the second little pig's doctor. He had faith that his patients could deal with the whole truth and that they should know what was behind the metrics. The doctor told the third little pig that his overall health was at risk—mostly due to his lifestyle. The doctor explained how weight, blood pressure, and cholesterol levels are pretty good indicators of health, but can't be used as the only ways to determine true health. A lot would depend on the little pig paying attention to his body and communicating with the doctor when things felt "funny." The little pig wondered what metric "feeling funny" was and the doctor explained that it wasn't a metric. It was simply the little pig talking to the doctor.

> *"So what do I do with the measures?"*
>
> *"You collect them, track them, and we use them as indicators to see if there's anything we're missing and if you're making progress."*
>
> *"So, I have to improve these numbers?" the pig asked as he took the chart.*
>
> *"No. You have to get healthy. Those numbers will just give us an idea if you're on the right track."*
>
> *The third little pig snorted. "What's the difference?"*
>
> *"Well, there are many indicators. Blood pressure, weight, and cholesterol levels are just three. I do want you to improve these areas, but not at the cost of other areas, such as how well you sleep, if you get enough exercise, stress tests, memory, nutrition, etc. The goal is to be healthy—not only clinically, but emotionally."*
>
> *"So, I don't have to improve these numbers?"*
>
> *"No, you could feasibly get healthier without improving some of those specific measures."*

"So, what's the plan?"

"Good question, little pig!" The doctor laid out a simple improvement plan for the little pig. He also showed the third little pig how to take his blood pressure, weight, and cholesterol levels. He had the little pig fill out a daily journal and a weekly online diary. The weekly online diary included the data he collected, a "how I feel today" meter, and a section where he was supposed to log what he had done that week to get healthy. The doctor promised to check the online diary, and if there was anything that seemed out of place, he'd contact the little pig.

"I hope you don't think I'm micro-managing you," the doctor said. "I just want to keep informed on your progress. It's very important to me that you get healthy."

"No, I like it," the third little pig said, knowing that his doctor cared. "But why don't you give me a whole battery of tests every month?"

"That's more than we need. I wouldn't put you through all those tests unless something in the measures indicates a need for it. That way I don't waste your time or your money."

By the six-month mark, the third little pig was looking better, feeling better, and based on his doctor's evaluation, doing better. By the ninth month, he was doing great. He looked really good. He garnered a lot of compliments from friends and coworkers. He was on his way.

The End

I'm sure my version won't become an accepted sequel to the traditional fable, but it served its purpose. My daughter fell asleep about halfway through.

Data

We'll start with some basic terms that will allow us to communicate more clearly. Data, measures, information, and metrics are distinctly different, but fully intertwined entities. Each builds upon the other. Metrics are made up of other metrics and information. Information is made up of measures, and measures are comprised of data.

Figure 2-1 illustrates disparate entities that many times are mistakenly associated with or thought of as metrics.

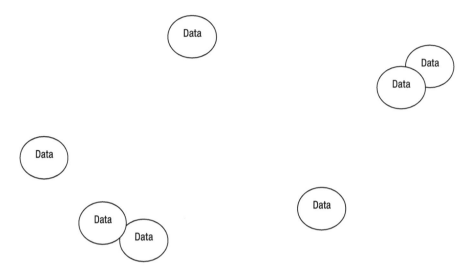

Figure 2-1. Data relationship map

Data is most commonly defined as "individual facts, statistics, or items of informa-tion." This definition, however, is overly generous. It implies accuracy. Moreover, it implies a level of usefulness that is not inherently present in data. Data, for our purposes, is the simplest form of information possible and is usually represented by a number or value; for example: six, twenty-two, seventy, true, false, high, or low. By itself, data is essentially useless because it fails to relate any meaning-ful information. As in Figure 2-1, some data can be "related" as represented by overlapping bubbles, but this is not part of the definition of data.

Data is the simplest form of information possible. It is usually represented by a number or value.

Data can be wildly unrelated (the bubbles far apart) or they can be correlated through a common purpose. When analyzing data, a relationship map can pro-vide a visual representation of the data's relationship to other data. Many times a relationship is mistakenly assumed to exist between data because the data comes from a common source or was gathered with a single purpose in mind. For example, if we looked at "time to respond" and "time to resolve" data, they may seem to be related. The source may be the same—a trouble-ticket track-ing system. The type of data (time) may also give the impression it is related more than it is. Frequently sets of data, regardless of the source or purpose, are not related. Assuming there is a relationship among unrelated sets of data causes us to come to incorrect conclusions. Response and resolution times, for example, don't affect one another, and they communicate different things.

Measures

Figure 2-2 illustrates the next level of information: measures and how data is related.

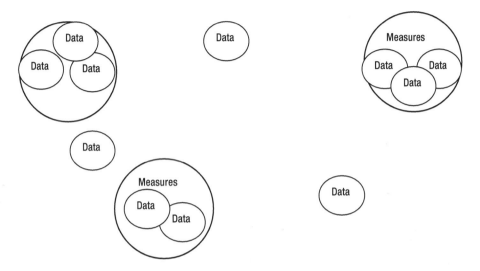

Figure 2-2. Measures and data relationship map

Measures begin to give us a more useful picture by incorporating some level of detail. The detail may include units of measure (in 50%, "percent" is the unit of measure and the data is 50) and information regarding how the data relates to other data. To state "70 percent" is more useful than to simply state "70." Even better, we may have "70 percent of 63 users." Each measure is made up of one or more datum. These measures, like the data, can have different levels of interrelations. One of the bubbles (top left in Figure 2-2) depicts a grouping of data that lacks a parent measure. This data is grouped because it is related, but it doesn't lead to a more meaningful measure. Demographics and height and weight are examples of this—data that may be useful, but doesn't necessarily feed into a larger measure.

Other data are floating independently within the map. These are rogue data (any term that means "no connections" works) that may or may not have a use later.

Measures bring more clarity to the data by grouping them in true relationships and adding a little context. Still, without clear connections to an underlying purpose or root question, measures are nothing more than dressed-up data.

Measures bring more clarity to the data by grouping them in true relationships and adding a little context.

Information

Figure 2-3 illustrates the first useful level of information—and that's just what we call it, "information." Information groups measures and data (as well as rogue data) into a meaningful capsule.

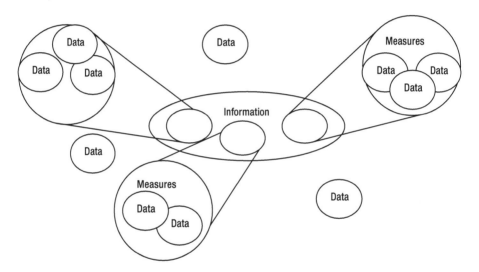

Figure 2-3. Data, measures, and information relationship map

Information takes measures and data and adds context. Notice that some data is not included in the information. Some data, regardless of how well it is collected, no matter how well you plan, may be superfluous. In the end, you may determine that the data does not fit or does not help to answer the root question you are working on. Information pulls in only the data and measures needed.

The context information brings to the data and measures is essential to moving indiscernible numerical points to an understandable state. With measures, we know that we are talking about percentages and that it is related to a number of users. Information adds context in the form of meaning, thus making the measures understandable: "Seventy percent of 63 users prefer the ski machine over the stair stepper."

Information adds context in the form of meaning, thus making the measures understandable.

While information within the right context can be especially useful, a metric may be what is truly needed.

Before we go on to the next piece of the puzzle, it may help to look at an example of how actual information (data and measures) fits into the diagram. Figure 2-4 shows an example using information around Speed to Resolve.

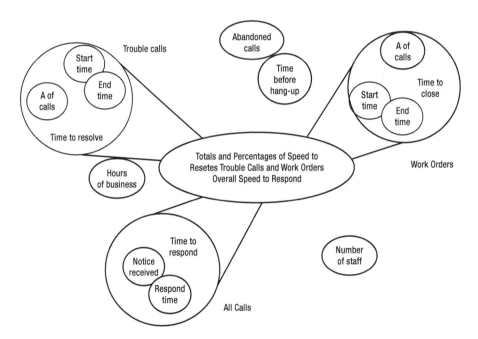

Figure 2-4. Speed to Resolve relationship map

Metrics

Figure 2-5 illustrates a full story, a metric. It's a picture made up of information, measures, and data. It should fulfill the adage, "a picture is worth a thousand words."

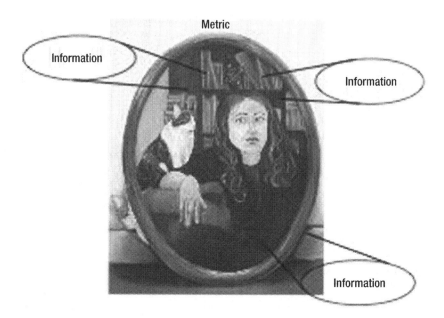

Figure 2-5. Metrics as a picture. Illustration by Alyssa Klubeck

We finally reach the all-important definition of "metric." A metric is more than simply grouping multiple pieces of information together. Well, not really much more.

A metric, by my definition, is made up of information, measures, and data. Metrics can also include other metrics. The main difference between metrics and information is that a metric tells a complete story, fully answering a root question. And it should tell the "right" story. If the metric tells the story completely wrong, it's not much use. Along with the data, measures, and information, the metric includes prose. While a picture may be worth a thousand words, a picture without an explanation is still open to multiple interpretations.

A metric tells a complete story, fully answering a root question.

If you've done a good job with the metric because your charts, graphs, and tables are telling a well-formed story, it will be much harder for misinterpretation. But, it's still possible. Unless you feel confident that those viewing your metrics don't have their own agendas, aren't likely to misinterpret, and are totally open-minded, I highly recommend rounding out the picture with words.

This need for prose is not a new concept. My daughter took an art appreciation class in college. I was not surprised to find that there was a textbook that accompanied the class. Each work of art had pages of text on the artist, some background on why the artist created it, the length of time it took to create it, the medium that was used, and the circumstances behind it becoming relevant. But all this shocked me because when I was in high school, I remember my art teacher explaining how art had no definitive meaning outside the way each viewer interpreted it. This was especially true of modern art (which I still don't understand). Rather than leave the interpretation to the audience, these textbooks had the all-important explanation of the message behind the painting spelled out right there. Each painting, sculpture, and drawing had one. Each etching, carving, and prehistoric wall-painting had one. An explanation of what the artist was trying to "tell" us with his thousand-word image.

If it's useful to explain the meaning behind a work of art, how much more necessary is it to capture the meaning of a metric? And wouldn't it be best to have the meaning explained by the artist herself? This explanation is, of course, an interpretation of the metric. It's true that if you ask five people to interpret a metric, you may get five different answers—but you'll want your interpretation to be the one presented with the picture. If metrics are used properly, your interpretation will not be taken as "truth," but for what it is: one way to view the meaning of the metric.

"Seventy percent of 63 users prefer the ski machine over the stair stepper for the aerobic portion of their exercise program. The wait time for the ski machine is 25 minutes on average. Typically, there is no wait time on the stair steppers. There are 3 ski machines and 12 stair steppers." This is getting close to being a "good" metric. If a picture (chart or graph) is added, it may get even closer. The goal of the metric is to tell a complete (and useful) story, in response to a root question.

The question is actually the driver of a good metric. You can't have a good metric without the root question. When we look at our ski machine vs. stair stepper metric, we don't know the usefulness of the metric because we don't know what the question is. We can jump to conclusions and worse, we can leap to a potentially regrettable decision.

Should we buy more ski machines? Get rid of some of the stair steppers? Should we make the limit for time on the ski machine less? Should we create an exercise class based on the stair stepper? It should be obvious that the proper answer is not obvious. Part of the confusion may be due to the lack of a question. Why did we collect the data? Why did we do the analysis that led us to the metric? It's impossible to tell a complete story without a root question.

Root Questions

In my book *Why Organizations Struggle So Hard to Improve So Little* (Praeger, 2009), my coauthors, Michael Langthorne and Donald Padgett, and I compare metrics to a tree. In this view, the data are the leaves, the measures are the twigs, the information is the branches, and the metrics are the trunk of the tree. All of these exist only with a good set of roots. These roots represent the root question. This analogy is a great way of showing the relationship between the components of the metric.

Figure 2-6 shows another view of the components that make up a metric. It's fitting that it looks like an organic structure.

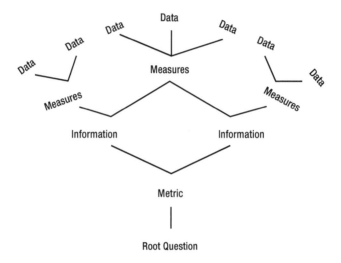

Figure 2-6. Metric components

Without a good root question, the answers that you derive may lead you in the wrong direction. Answers are only useful when you know the question. The root question is so integral to the metric that it has to be part of the definition of a metric.

A metric tells a complete story using data, measures, information, and other metrics to answer a root question.

The root question is essentially the most important component of a metric. It is the map we use to help determine our direction. It identifies the goal of our journey. There are instances where you may, with good reason and to good result, collect data without a root question, but for the practical use of metrics, this is unacceptable. It would be like taking off on a journey without a destination in mind. No purpose, no plan, and no direction—just get in your car and start driving.

Later you may realize that you forgot your driver's license, your money, and even your shoes. You may realize that you'd already traveled too far to make it back with the amount of fuel remaining in your tank. You may realize that the only logical course of action is to continue on, although you don't know where you will end up. You are more likely to end up where you don't want to be. Since the only right place would be the destination that you forgot to determine, it is much more likely that you will end up someplace other than that right place. And, when you fail to reach the destination (which in the end you may or may not have identified), you will blame the car. It didn't get enough miles to the gallon.

You won't blame the lack of forethought. Even if you get more gas *and* you figure out where you want to go, you'll not go back home for your wallet, license, or shoes. You've invested too much. Instead, you'll continue on and try to reach the destination from where you are, not wanting to admit that everything you'd done to that point was wasted effort.

If you're like most of us and need to make the most of what you have, embarking on this meandering journey is *more* than wasteful. The lack of direction will seed a level of despair and resentment in you and your coworkers, your superiors, and subordinates. It can destroy the spirit of your organization.

The root question provides you with focus and direction. You know where you are headed. You know the destination. You know the purpose of the metrics and the question you are trying to answer.

A correctly worded and fully thought-out root question, allows you to determine the right answer(s). Without a root question—*the right question*—the answer you derive will be the result of a meandering journey. This answer will likely do more harm than good.

Even a well-worded root question will fail to lead to good results if the question is not the *right* question.

To put it all together, let's look at a full example. A metric is a complete story told through representation of information. Information in turn, is a compilation of measures, used to convey meaning. Measures are the results built from data, the lowest level of collectable components (values or numbers). The following is a simple example:

- *Data*: 15 and 35

- *Measures*: 15 mpg and 35 mpg

- *Information*: Miles-per-gallon achieved using unleaded gasoline in a compact car: 15 mpg in the city, 35 mpg on the highway

- *Metric*: The metric that would logically follow would be a picture (charts or graphs in most cases) that tells a story. In this case the story may be a comparison between the fuel efficiency of different compact car models (miles per gallon), combined with other indicators used to select the right car for you.

- *Root Question*: What is the best car for me?

The use of data, measures, and information are more relative than hard and fast. I don't mean to dictate inflexible definitions that will keep you from getting to the metric. The goal is to develop metrics—answers—to our questions.

The data could include the miles-per-gallon tag. Measures could include "in the city" and "on the highway." Information could distinguish between the various cars' make and model. The major point to take away is that additional meaning (and context) are provided as we progress from data to measures to information. Also, metrics make a full story of this and much more information.

The metric, like its components, are tools that can be used to answer the root question. We will address the proper use of these tools later. For now, it's enough to have a common understanding of what the components are and how they relate to each other.

The Data-Metric Paradox

There is an interesting paradox involving the components of metrics and their relationship to the root question used to derive them.

Data, the easiest to understand, identify, and collect, should be the last item to develop. The most complex and difficult component, the root question, has to come first. As our analogy of the hapless driver on the meandering journey showed, we must first identify our destination and purpose. Rather than start with the simple to build the complex, we must start with the most complex and use it to identify the simple.

The three little pigs also ran into this paradox. The first pig's doctor was happy with data and measures, but ignored the bigger, more important requirement. He lost his patient, but did it with "healthy" numbers. Business can do the same. You can have good data points (sales per customer, profit/sale, or repeat customers) and still go out of business.

We have to start with the complex to uncover the simple—start at the root question and drive unerringly toward data.

The best way to create a metric is to move from the question to the metric to the information to the measures and, finally, to the data.

Unfortunately, most times we attempt it in the opposite direction, starting with the simple (data) trying to expound on it to develop the complex (root question). This process seldom succeeds. But when we start at the complex, forming a picture of what the question is and how the answer will look, it becomes easy to work down to the data.

Data, measures, information, and metrics all serve the same master: the root question. They all have a common goal: to provide answers to the question. Because of this, the question defines the level of answer necessary.

Let's pose the following question: How far is it to Grandma's house? You don't need a metric to provide the answer to this question. You don't even need information. A measure (for example, the number of miles) will suffice. And you will be fully satisfied. For data to be sufficient, you have to ask the question with enough context to make a simple number or value an adequate answer. How many miles is it to Grandma's house? How much longer will it take to get to Grandma's house? In these cases, data is all you need. But data is rarely useful in and of itself.

Let's pose another question: Do we have time to do any sightseeing or shopping along the way and still make it in time for Grandma's turkey dinner? To answer this, we require information. The measures and data might include the following:

- The time Grandma is serving dinner
- The current time
- The number of sightseeing or shopping stops along the way
- The estimated time to sightsee/shop per stop

The root question will determine the level of the answer. If the question is complex enough and needs answers on a periodic basis, chances are you will need to develop a comprehensive metric. A question along the lines of "How is the health of (a service or little pigs)?" may require a metric to answer it, especially if you want to continue to monitor the health on a regular basis.

The vagueness of the question makes it more complex. Clarity simplifies.

When designing a metric, the most important part is getting the right root question. This will let us know what level of information is required to answer it. It will govern the design of the metric down to what data to collect.

Metric Components

Let's recap the components of a metric and their definitions:

- *Data*: Data, for our purposes, is the simplest possible form of information and is usually represented by a number or value; for example, six, twenty-two, seventy, true, false, high, or low.

- *Measures*: Made up of data, measures add the lowest level of context possible to the data. Measures can be made up of other measures.

- *Information*: Information is made up of data and measures. Information can be made up of other information. Information provides additional, more meaningful context.

- *Metrics*: Metrics are made up of data, measures, and information. Metrics can be made up of other metrics. Metrics give full context to the information. Metrics (attempt to) tell a complete story. Metrics (attempt to) answer a root question.

- *Root Question*: The purpose for the metric. Root questions define the requirements of the metric and determine its usefulness.

Recap

This chapter introduced a common language for metrics and their components. It also introduced the Data-Metric Paradox, in which we learned that we have to start with the most complex to drive to the simple. We have to start with the root question to get us safely to the proper level of information necessary to answer the question. It's possible the question may not require a metric, or even information. When tasked by management to create a metric (or a metric program) we have to slow down and ask what the root questions are. We have to be willing and able to accept that the answer may not lie in creating a metric at all.

Designing and Documenting Your Metrics

The How

Now that we have a common language, the next step is to discuss how to proceed. I've read numerous books, articles, and blog posts on Balanced Scorecards, Performance Measures, and Metrics for Improvement. I haven't found one yet that puts "how to develop a metric from scratch" into plain English. It's about time someone did.

In this chapter we'll cover the following:

- How to form a root question—the right root question
- How to develop a metric by drawing a picture
- How to flesh out the information, measures, and data needed to make the picture
- How to collect data, measures, and information

This may seem like a lot of work (and it is), but I guarantee you that if you follow this method you will save an enormous amount of time and effort in the long run. Most of your savings will come from less rework, less frustration, and less dissatisfaction with the metrics you develop.

Think of it this way: You can build a house by first creating a blueprint to ensure you get the house that you want. Or you can just order a lot of lumber and supplies and make it up as you go along. This process doesn't work when building a house or developing software. It requires discipline to do the groundwork first. It will be well worth it. I've never seen anyone disappointed because they had a well thought-out plan, but I've helped many programmers try to unravel the spaghetti code they ended up with because they started programming before they knew what the requirements were.

While programmers have improved at upfront planning, and builders would never think to just start hammering away, sadly those seeking to use metrics still want to skip the requirements phase.

So let's start working on that blueprint.

Getting to the Root Question

Before you can design a metric, you have to first identify the root question: What is the real driving need? The discussion I've had many times with clients often goes like the following dialog (in which I'm the metrics designer):

> Director: "I'd like to know if our service desk is responsive to our customers."

The first clue that the metrics designer has to dig deeper for the real root question is that the answer to the given question could be yes or no.

> Metrics Designer: "What do you mean by responsive?"

> Director: "Are we answering calls in a timely manner?"

> Metrics Designer: "What exactly is a 'timely manner'? Do you mean how many seconds it takes or how many times the phone rings?"

> Director: "I guess within the first three rings?"

The designer made a note—that the director guessed calls should be answered within three rings, but that end users had to provide the actual definition of "responsiveness."

> Metrics Designer: "Okay. Why do we need to know this? What's driving the curiosity?"

> Director: "I've had some complaints that we aren't picking up the phone quickly enough. Customers say they can't reach us or they have to wait too long to get to speak to a person."

Metrics Designer: "What constitutes 'not quick enough'? Or, what is a wait that is 'too long'?"

Director: "I don't know."

The designer made some more notes. The director was willing to admit that he didn't know what the customer meant by "quick enough" and that he didn't know what would please the customer. This admission was helpful.

Metrics Designer: "I suggest we ask some of your customers to determine these parameters. This will help us determine expectations and acceptable ranges. But we also need to know what you want to know. Why do you want to know how responsive the service desk is?"

Director: "Well, the service desk is the face of our organization—when most customers say 'Emerald City Services' they think of the service desk."

Metrics Designer: "So, what do you want to know about the face of your organization?"

Director: "How well it's received by our customers. I want to know if it's putting forth a good image."

This is a much better starting point for our metric design. With the root question (How well is the service desk representing Emerald Services?) we can decide on a more meaningful picture—a picture that encompasses everything that goes into answering the question.

There are other possible results of our inquisition. Our job is to reach the root question. We have to help our clients determine what their real underlying needs are and what they need or want to know. One tool for doing so is the Five Whys.

The Five Whys is simple in its concept. You ask "why" five times, until the client can no longer answer with a deeper need. Of course, you can't ask "why" repeatedly like a child being told they can't play in the rain. You have to ask it in a mature manner. Many times you don't actually use the word, "why." As in the earlier example, sometimes you ask using other terms—like "what" and "how" and "what if?"

The process isn't so much predicated on the use of the word "why" as it is grounded in attempting to reach the root purpose or need. Perhaps the worst error is to jump happily at the first "why" in which you feel some confidence that you could answer. We are *all* problem solvers by nature, and the possibility of latching onto a question with which we can easily provide an answer is very tempting.

Start with Goals

If you don't have a list of goals for your unit, you can add value by first developing them. This may seem to be outside of the process for designing metrics, but since you must have a good root question to move forward, if you have to create metrics around goals, you don't have any choice.

If you have a set of goals, then your task becomes much easier. But be careful; the existence of a documented strategic plan does not mean you have usable goals. Unless you have a living strategic plan, one that you are actually following, the strategic plan you have is probably more of an ornament for your shelf than a usable plan. But, let's start with the assumption that you'll have to identify your goals, improvement opportunities, and/or problems.

The best way I've found to get to the root questions when starting from a blank slate is to hold a working session with a trained facilitator, your team, and yourself. This shouldn't take longer than two or three one-hour sessions.

When building metrics from a set of goals, work with the goals (as you would a root question) to get to the overarching goal. Many strategic plans are full of short- to mid-range goals. You want to get to the parent goal. You need to identify the long range goals, the mission, and/or the vision. You need to know why the lower-level goals exist, so that if the strategic plan doesn't include the parent goal, you'll have to work with the team to determine it. Again, the Five Whys will work.

We've discussed using five "whys" to get to a root need and to get to driving goal behind a strategic plan. However, any method for eliciting requirements should work. The important thing is to get to the underlying need. The root question should address what needs to be achieved, improved, or resolved (at the highest level possible).

What's important to remember is that you can work from wherever you start back to a root question and then forward again to the metric (if necessary). I told a colleague that I wanted to write a book on metrics.

> *"Why? Don't you have enough to do?" She knew I was perpetually busy.*

> *"Yes, but every time I turn around, I run into people who need help with metrics," I answered.*

> *"Why a book?" She was good at The Five Whys.*

> *"It gives me a tool to help teach others. I can tell them to read the book and I'll be able to reference it."*

> *"So, you want to help others with designing metrics. That's admirable. What else will you need to do?"*

And that started me on a brainstorming journey. I captured ideas from presenting speeches, teaching seminars and webinars, to writing articles and proposing curriculum for colleges. I ended up with a larger list of things to accomplish than just a book. I also got to the root need and that helped me focus on why I wanted to write the book. That helps a lot when I feel a little burned out or exhausted. It helps me to persevere when things aren't going smoothly. It helps me think about measuring success, not based on finishing the book (although that's a sub-measure I plan on celebrating) but on the overall goal of helping others develop solid and useful metrics programs.

Once you think you have the root question, chances are you'll need to edit it a little. I'm not suggesting that you spend hours making it "sound" right. It's not going to be framed and put over the entrance. No, I mean that you have to edit it for clarity. It has to be exact. The meaning has to be clear. As you'll see shortly, you'll test the question to ensure it is a root—but beforehand it will help immensely if you've defined every component of the question to ensure clarity.

Define the terms—even the ones that are obvious. Clarity is paramount.

Keep in mind, most root questions are very short, so it shouldn't take too much effort to clearly define each word in the question.

As with many things, an example may be simpler. Based on the conversation on why I wanted to write this book, let's assume a possible root question is: How effective is this book at helping readers design metrics? You can ensure clarity by defining the words in the question.

1. **How effective** is this book at helping readers design metrics?

    a. What do we mean by effective? In this case, since it's my goal, I'll do the definitions.

    b. The how portion means, which parts of the book are helpful? Which parts aren't? Also, does it enable someone to develop high-quality metrics? After all, my goal is to make this book a practical tool and guide for developing a metrics program. "How well can the reader design metrics after reading the book?

2. How effective **is this book** at helping readers design metrics?

   a. Do we really want to measure the effectiveness of the book or is there something else you want to measure?

   b. Even obvious definitions, like this one—may lead you to modify the question. If asked, "What do you mean by this book?" I might very well answer, "Oh, actually I want to know if the system is effective, of which the book is the vehicle for sharing." This would lead us to realize that I really wanted to know if my system worked for others—more so than if this form of communication was effective.

3. How effective is this book **at helping readers** design metrics?

   c. Does it *help*? I have to define if "*help*" means

      i. Can the reader develop metrics after reading it?

      ii. Is the reader better at developing metrics after reading it?

      iii. Does the reader avoid the mistakes I preach against?

   d. *Readers* are another obvious component—but we could do some more clarification.

      i. Does "reader" mean someone who reads the "whole" book or someone who reads any part of the book?

      ii. Is the reader based on the target audience?

4. How effective is this book at helping readers **design metrics**?

   a. What do I mean by "design"? As you have read, for me designing a metric involves a lot more than the final metric. It includes identifying the root need and then ensuring a metric is the proper way to answer it. So, while "design" may mean development, it has to be taken in the context of the definition of a metric.

b. What do I mean by metric? Do I mean the metric part of the equation or does it include the whole thing—root question, metric, information, measures, and data? If you'd read the book already, you'd know the answer to this question. The metric cannot be done properly without the root question, and is made up of information, measures, data, and other metrics. Even with that—what I mean in the root question may be a little different than this because the outcome of following the process may be to not create a metric. In that case, using the root question to provide an answer would be a success—although no metric was designed.

Based on this exercise, if I chose to keep the root question the same, I'd now know much better how to draw the picture. Chances are though, after analyzing each word in the question, I would rewrite the question. The purpose behind my question was to determine if the book was successful. And since success could result in not designing metrics, I would rewrite my question to be more in tune with what I actually deem success—the effective use of my system. The new root question might be: How effective is my system in helping people who want or need to design metrics?

Testing the Root Question

If you think you've got the root question identified, you're ready to proceed. Of course, it may be worthwhile to test the question to see if you've actually succeeded.

Test 1. Is the "root" question actually asking for information, measures, or data? "I'd like to know the availability of system X." This request begs us to ask, "Why?" There is an underlying need or requirement behind this seemingly straightforward question. When you dig deep enough, you'll get to the real need, which is simply a request for data. The root question should *not* be a direct request for data. The following are examples of requests for data: Do we have enough gas to reach our destination? Is the system reliable or do we need a backup? How long will it take to complete the project?

Test 2. Is the answer to the question going to be simple? Is it going to be a measure? Data? If the answers are either "yes" or "no," chances are you're not there yet or the question doesn't require a metric to provide an answer. It may seem too easy—that you wouldn't get questions after all this work that could be answered with a yes or no. But, it happens. It may mean only a little rework on the question, but that rework is still necessary. Is our new mobile app going to be a best seller? Should we outsource our IT department? Are our employees satisfied? These may seem like good root questions, but, they can all be answered with a simple yes or no.

Test 3. How will the answer be used? If you've identified a valid root question, you will have strong feelings, or a clear idea of how you will use the answer. The answer should provide discernible benefits. Let's take my question about the effectiveness of this book at helping readers develop metrics. If I learn that it's highly effective at helping readers, what will I do? I may use the information to gain opportunities for speaking engagements based on the book. I may submit the book to be considered for a literary award. I may have to hold a celebration. If the answer is that the book is ineffective, then I may investigate possible means of correcting the situation. I may have to offer handbooks/guidelines on how to use the book. I may have to offer more information via a web site. If the feedback is more neutral, I may look at ways to improve in a later edition.

The key is to have predefined expectations of what you will do with the answers you'll receive. When I ask a client how they'll use the answer, if I get a confused stare or their eyes gloss over, I know we're not there yet.

Test 4. Who will the answer be shared with? Who will see the metric? If the answer is only upper management, then chances are good that you need to go back to the drawing board. If you've reached the root question, many more people should benefit from seeing the answer. One key recipient of the answer should be the team that helped you develop it. If it's only going to be used to appease upper management—chances are you haven't gotten to the root *or* the answer won't require a metric.

Test 5. Can you draw a picture using it? When you design the metric, you will do it much more as an art than a science. There are lots of courses you can take on statistical analysis. You can perform exciting and fun analysis using complex mathematical tools. But, I'm not covering that here. We're talking about how to develop a useable metrics program—a tool for improvement. If you can't draw a picture as the answer for the question, it may not be a root question.

Not all root questions will pass these tests.

I'm not saying that all root questions *must* pass these tests. But, all root questions that require a "metric" to answer them must. If your question doesn't pass these tests, you have some choices.

1. Develop the answer without using data, measures, information, or metrics. Sometimes the answer is a process change. Sometimes the answer is to stop doing something, do it differently, or start doing something new. It doesn't have to result in measuring at all.

2. Develop the answer using measures (or even just data). This may be a one-time measure. You may not need to collect or report the data more than once.

3. Work on the question until it passes the five tests—so you can then develop a metric. Why would you want to rework your question simply to get to a metric? You shouldn't. If you feel confident about the result, stop. If the client says you've hit upon the root question, stop. If the question resonates fully, stop. Wherever you are, that's where you'll be. Work from there. *Don't force a metric if it's not required.*

Your task is *not* to develop a metric—it's to determine the root question and provide an answer.

Developing a Metric

It's an interesting argument: is the process of designing metrics a science or an art? If you read statistics textbooks, you might take the side of science. If you read *Transforming Performance Measurement: Rethinking the Way We Measure and Drive Organizational Success* by Dean Spitzer (AMACON, 2007), or *How To Measure Anything* by Douglas Hubbard (Wiley, 2010), you might argue that it's an art. I propose, like most things in real life (vs. theory), it's a mixture of both.

One place it's more art than science is in the *design* of a metric. I can say this without reservation because to design our metric, you want to actually draw a picture. It's not fine art. It's more like the party game where you're given a word or phrase and you have to draw a picture so your teammates are able to guess what the clue is.

At the first seminar I taught on designing metrics, "Do-It-Yourself Metrics", I broke the students into groups of four or five. After stepping through the exercise for identifying root questions, I told them to draw a picture to provide an answer to a question. The question was, "How do we divide our team's workload to be the most productive?" Figure 3-1 shows the best of the students' answers.

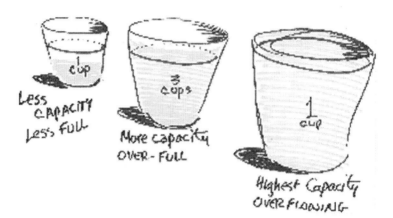

Figure 3-1. Workload division metric

This picture shows how each person (represented by a different cup) has different levels of work. The level of the liquid represents the amount of work "in each person's cup." The line near the top is the highest level the liquid should be poured to, because the froth will cause it to overflow. This line represents the most each person can actually handle, leaving room at the top for the "extra"—like illness, lunch, vacation, etc. By looking at the picture, the manager gets an easy-to-understand story of who has too much work, who can take on more, who is more productive, and who needs to improve their skill sets so that they can eventually have a larger cup.

A useful part of drawing the picture was clarity around the question. To ensure that we drew it right, we needed to also define the terms we were using in the picture: productivity, workload, and team.

Define the terms—even the ones that are obvious. Here too, clarity is paramount.

We found out that workers A, B, and C made up the team—they did the same type of work in a small unit of the organization. We also learned that the word "team" didn't mean that the group normally worked together. On the contrary, this "team" worked independently on different tasks. This simple realization gave the manager more ideas.

Workload was defined as the tasks given to the workers by the manager. It excluded many other tasks the workers accomplished for other people in the organization, customers, and each other. The only tasks that counted in this picture were the ones with deadlines and accountability to the management chain.

Productivity was defined as how many tasks were completed on time (or by the deadline).

These definitions are essential to developing the "right" metric. We could have drawn a good picture and designed a metric without these clarifications, but we would have risked measuring the wrong things.

Don't assume the terms used in the question are understood.

The metric would also be useful later, when the manager provided training opportunities for the staff. If the training did what was expected, the cups would increase in size—perhaps from a 32-ounce to a 44-ounce super size.

Does this seem strange? Does it seem too simple?

While I can't argue against things being "strange," very few things are ever "too simple." Einstein once said, "Make it as simple as possible, but no simpler." This is not too simple—like Goldilocks was fond of saying, "it's just right."

Once we have clear definitions for the terms that make up the root question, we will have a much better picture! Remember the importance of a common language? It is equally important that everyone fully understands the language used to create the root question.

I work with clients to modify these drawings until it provides the full answer to their question. This technique has excellent benefits. By using a picture:

- It's easier to avoid jumping to data. This is a common problem. Remember the natural tendency to go directly to data.

- It's easier to think abstractly and avoid being put in a box. Telling someone to "think outside the box" is not always an effective way to get them to do so.

- We avoid fears, uncertainty, or doubt about the ability to collect, analyze, and report the necessary information. These common emotions toward metrics restrict your ability to think creatively and thoroughly. They tend to "settle" for less than the ideal answer.

- We have a non-threatening tool for capturing the needs. No names, no data or measures. No information that would worry the client. No data at all. Just a picture. Of course this picture may change drastically by the time you finalize the metric. This is essentially a tool for creatively thinking without being restricted by preconceptions of what a metric (or what a particular answer) should be.

One key piece of advice is not to design your metric in isolation. Even if you are your own metric customer, involve others. I am not advocating the use of a consultant. I am advocating the use of someone—anyone—else. You need someone to help you generate ideas and to bounce your ideas off of. You need someone to help you ask "why." You need someone to discuss your picture with (and perhaps to draw it). This is a creative, inquisitive process—and for most of us, it is immensely easier to do this with others. Feel free to use your whole team. But don't do it alone.

A good root question will make the drawing easier.

Having a complete picture drawn (I don't mean a Picasso) makes the identification of information, measures, and data not only easy, but ensures you have a good chance of getting the right components.

The picture has to be "complete." After I have something on paper (even if it's stick figures), I ask the client, "what's missing?" "Does this fully answer your question?" Chances are, it won't. When I did the conference seminar, the team members had cups—but they were all the same size and there was no "fill-to-here line." After some discussion and questioning, the group modified the drawing to show the full story.

It's actually fun to keep modifying the picture, playing with it until you feel it is complete. People involved start thinking about what they want and need instead of what they think is possible. This is the real power of drawing the metric.

Identifying the Information, Measures, and Data Needed

Only after you have a complete picture do you address the components. This picture is an abstract representation of the answer(s) to our root question. It's like an artist's rendition for the design of a cathedral—the kind used in marketing the idea to financial backers. When you present the idea to potential donors, you don't need to provide them with blueprints, you need to pitch the concept.

Next are the specific design elements to ensure the building will be feasible. As the architect, you can provide the artist's conception and do so while knowing from experience whether the concept is sound. Your next step is to determine what will go into the specific design—the types of structures, wiring, plumbing, and load-bearing walls. Then you will have to determine the materials you need to make it a reality—what do we need to fill in the metric?

Let's look at the workload example. How do we divide our team's workload to be the most productive? Remember, the picture is of drink cups—various sizes from 20-ounce, to 32-ounce, to a super-sized 44-ounce. Each cup has a mark that designates the "fill" level—and if we fill above this line, the froth will overflow the cup. Using the picture, we need to determine the following:

- How do we measure our team's level of productivity?

- How do we currently allocate (divide) the work?

- What are other ways to allocate the work?

Of the three pieces of information listed, only the first seems to need measures. The other two are process definitions. Since our question is driven by a goal (to improve the team's productivity), the process for designing the metric will produce other useful elements toward the goal's achievement.

Information can be made up of other information, measures, and data. It isn't important to delineate each component—what's important is to work from the complex to the simple without rushing. Don't jump to the data!

An example of how you can move from a question to measures and then to data follows.

- How do we measure our team's level of productivity?

  - How much can each worker do?

    - Worker A?

    - Worker B?

    - Worker C?

  - How much does each worker do?

    - By worker (same breakout as the previous measure)

  - How much does each worker have in his or her cup?

    - By worker

  - How long does it take to perform a task?

    - By worker

    - By type of task

    - By task

I logged a sub-bullet for each worker to stress what seems to be anti-intuitive to many people—most times there is no "standard" for everyone. When developing measures, I find it fascinating how many clients want to set a number that they think will work for everyone.

Machinery, even manufactured to painstakingly precise standards, doesn't function identically. Why do we think that humans—the most complex living organism known, and with beautiful variety—would fit a standardized behavior pattern?

Of course it would be easier if we had a standard—as in the amount of work that can be done by a programmer and the amount of work each programmer does. But this is unlikely.

You may also be curious why we have the first and second measures—how much a worker can do and how much he accomplishes. But since the goal is to increase the productivity of the team, the answer may not be in reallocating the load—it may be finding ways to get people to work to their potential. A simpler reason is that we don't know if each worker is being given as much as they can do—or too much.

Looking back at Figure 3-1, we may need to decide if the flavor of drink matters. Do we need to know the type of work each worker has to do? Does the complexity of the work matter? Does the customer matter? Does the purpose of the work matter? Does the quality of the work matter? Should we only be measuring around the manager's assigned work? If we exclude other work, do we run the risk of improving productivity in one area at the cost of others?

These questions are being asked at the right time—compared with if we started with the data. If we started with a vague idea (instead of a root question) and jumped to the data—we'd be asking these questions after collecting reams of data, perhaps analyzing them and creating charts and graphs. Only when we showed the fruits of our labor to the client would we find out if we were on the right track.

I want to help you avoid wasting your time and resources. I want to convince you to build your metrics from a position of knowledge.

Collecting Measures and Data

Now that we've identified the information needed (and measures that make up that information) we need to collect the data. This is a lot easier with the question, metric picture (answer), and information already designed. The trick here is not to leave out details.

It's easy to skip over things or leave parts out because we assume it's obvious. Building on the workload example, let's look at some of the data we'd identify.

First we'll need task breakdowns so we know what the "work" entails. What comprises the tasks—so we can measure what tasks each worker "can" do. With this breakdown, we also need classifications for the types of tasks/work. When trying to explain concepts, I find it helpful to use concrete examples. The more abstract the concept, the more concrete the example should be.

> Task 1: Provide second-level support
>
> Task 1a: Analyze issue for cause
>
> Task 1b: Determine solution set
>
> Task 1c: Select best solution

This example would be categorized as "support." Other categories of a task may include innovation, process improvement, project development, or maintenance.

We'll also need a measure of how long it takes each worker to perform each task, as seen in Table 3-1.

Table 3-1. Amount of Time Workers Perform Tasks

Worker	Task 1	Task 2
A	1 hr average	15 minutes average
B	1.5 hrs average	30 minutes average
C	1.6 hrs average	28 minutes average

If we have measures for the work components, we should be able to roll this data "up" to determine how long it takes to do larger units of work.

Next, we'll need measures of what is assigned currently to each worker.

Worker A is working on support while workers B and C are working on maintenance.

Since we need to know what each worker is capable of ("can do") we will need to know the skill set of each worker. With specific identification of what they "can't" do. Many times we find the measure of X can be determined in part (or fully) by the measure of the inverse value $1/x$.

Worker A is not capable of doing maintenance work. That's why he isn't assigned to maintenance and does the support-level work instead.

Again, it's a lot easier once we work from the top down. Depending on the answers we would perform investigations to ensure the assumptions we come to are correct. Then we can make changes (improvements) based on these results.

Worker A wants to do more maintenance-type tasks, but doesn't feel confident in her abilities to do so. The manager chose to develop a comprehensive training program for Worker A.

Workers B and C showed they had the skills necessary to provide support, and were willing to do so. The manager divided the support work more evenly between the team.

These types of adjustments (and new solutions) could be made throughout, depending on the answers derived from the metrics.

It was not necessary to be "perfect" in the identification of all measures and data. If you are missing something, that should become evident when trying to build the information and, finally, the metric. If you're missing something, it will stand out. If you have data or measures that you don't need, this, too, will become quickly evident when you put it all together for the metric.

You're not trying to be perfect out of the gate, but you definitely want to be as effective as possible. You'd like to be proactive and work from a strong plan. This happens when you use the root question and metric as your starting point.

It is truly amazing to see how a picture—not charts and graphs, but a creative drawing depicting the answer—works. It helps focus your efforts and keeps you from chasing data.

The metric "picture" provides focus, direction, and helps us avoid chasing data.

How to Collect Data

Once we've designed what the metric will look like, and have an idea of what information, measures, and data we'll need to fill it out, we need to discuss how to gather the needed parts. I'm not going to give you definitive steps as much as provide guidelines for collecting data. These "rules of thumb" will help you gather the data in as accurate a manner as possible.

Later, we'll expand on some of the factors that make the accuracy of the data uncertain. This is less a result of the mechanisms used and more a consequence of the amount of trust that the data providers have with you and management.

Use Automated Data When Possible

When I see a "Keep Out, No Trespassing" sign, I think of metrics. A no-trespassing sign is designed to keep people out of places that they don't belong. Many times it's related to safety. In the case of collecting data, you want to keep people out.

Why? The less human interaction with the data, the better. The less interaction, the more accurate the data will be, and the higher level of confidence everyone can have in its accuracy. Whenever I can collect the data through automated means, I do so. For example, to go back to the example in Chapter 2, rather than have someone count the number of ski machine or stair stepper users, I'd prefer to have some automated means of gathering this data. If each user has to log in information on the machine (weight, age, etc.) to use the programming features, the machine itself may be able to provide user data.

The biggest risk with using automated data may be the abundance and variety. If you find the exercise machines can provide the data you are looking for (because you worked from the question to the metric, down to the information and finally measures/data), great! But normally you also find a lot of other data not related to the metric. Any automated system that provides your data will invariably also provide a lot of data you aren't looking for.

For example, you'll have data on the demographics I already listed (age and weight). You'll also have data on the length of time users are on the machines, as well as the exercise program(s) selected; the users' average speed; and the total "distance" covered in the workout. The machine may also give information on average pulse rate. But, if none of this data serves the purpose of answering your root question, none of it is useful.

In our workload example, it will be difficult to gather data about the work without having human interaction. Most work accounting systems are heavily dependent on the workers capturing their effort, by task and category of work.

Beware!

So what happens when your client finds out about all of this untapped data?

He'll want to find a use for it! It's human nature to want to get your money's worth. And since you are already providing a metric, the client may also want you to find a place for some of this "interesting" data in the metric you're building. This risk is manageable and may be worth the benefit of having highly accurate data.

The risk of using automated data is that management will want to use data that has no relation to your root question, just because this extra data is available.

You should also be careful of over-trusting automated data. Sometimes the data only seems to be devoid of human intervention. What if the client wants to use the weight and age data collected in the ski machine? Well, the weight may have been taken by the machine and be devoid of human interaction (besides humans standing on the machine), but age is human-provided data, since the user of the machine has to input this data.

Employ Software and Hardware

Collecting data using software or hardware are the most common forms of automated data collection. I don't necessarily mean software or hardware developed for the purpose of collecting data (like a vehicle traffic counter). I mean something more like the ski-machine, equipment designed to provide a service with the added benefit of providing data on the system. Data collected automatically provides a higher level of accuracy, but runs the risk of offering too much data to choose from. Much of the data I use on a daily basis comes from software and hardware—including data on usage and speed.

Conduct Surveys

Surveys are probably the most common data-gathering tool. They are used in research (Gallup Polls), predictive analysis (exit polls during elections), feedback gathering (customer satisfaction surveys), marketing analysis (like the surveyors walking in shopping malls, asking for a few minutes of your time) and demographic data gathering (the US census). Surveys are used whenever you want to gather a lot of data from a lot of people—people being a key component. Surveys, by nature, involve people.

The best use of surveys is when you are seeking the opinions of the respondents. Any time you collect data by "asking" someone for information, the answer will lack objectivity. In contrast to using automated tools for collecting (high/total objectivity), surveys by nature are highly/totally subjective. So, the best use of the survey is when you purposefully want subjectivity.

Customer satisfaction surveys are a good example of this. Another is marketing analysis. If you want to know if someone likes one type of drink over another, a great way to find out is to ask. Surveys, in one way or another, collect your opinion. I lump all such data gathering under surveys—even if you don't use a "survey tool" to gather them. So, focus groups, and interviews fit under surveys. We'll cover the theories behind the types of surveys and survey methods later.

Use People

So far I've recommended avoiding human provision of data when accuracy is essential. I've also said that when you want an opinion, you want (have) to use humans. But, how about when you decide to use people for gathering data other than opinions? What happens when you use people because you can't afford an automated solution or an automated solution doesn't exist?

I try to stay fit and get to the gym on a regular basis. I've noticed that a gym staff member often walks around the facility with a log sheet on a clipboard. He'll visually count the number of people on the basketball courts. He'll then take a count of those using the aerobic machines. Next, the free weights, the weight machines, and finally the elevated track. He'll also check the locker room, and a female coworker will check the women's locker room.

How much human error gets injected into this process? Besides simply miscounting, it is easy to imagine how the counter can miss or double-count people. During his transition between rooms, areas, and floors of the facility, the staff member is likely to miss patrons and/or count someone more than once (for example, Gym-User A is counted while on the basketball court, and by the time the staffer gets to the locker room, Gym-User A is in the locker room, where he is counted again). Yet, it's not economically feasible to utilize automated equipment to count the facility's usage by area.

We readily accept the inherent inaccuracy in the human-gathered form of data collection. Thus we must ask the following:

- How critical is it to have a high degree of accuracy in our data?

- Is high accuracy worth the high cost?

- How important is it to have the data at all? If it's acceptable to simply have some insight into usage of the areas, a rough estimate may be more than enough

Many times you collect data using humans because we need human interaction to deal with the situation that generates the data. A good example is the IT help desk. Since you choose to have a human answer the trouble call (vs. an automated system), much of the data collected (and later used to analyze trends and predict problem areas) is done by the person answering the phone. Even an "automated" survey tool (e-mails generated and sent to callers) is dependent on the technician correctly capturing each phone caller's information.

Documenting Your Metrics

Now that you've designed your metric, you need to document it. Not only what you'll measure, but how.

In *Why Organizations Struggle So Hard to Improve So Little,* my coauthors and I addressed the need for structure and rigor in documenting work with metrics. More than any other organizational development effort, metrics require meticulous care. Excellent attention to detail is needed—not only in the information you use within the metric (remember the risks of human involvement), but also with the process involved.

In this chapter, we'll cover identifying the many possible components of a metric development plan and documenting the metric development plan so that it becomes a tool for not only the creation of the metric, but a tool for using it effectively.

The Components of a Well-Documented Metric

Besides documenting the components of the metric—data, measures, information, pictures, and of course, the root question we will also need to capture how these components are collected, analyzed, and reported. This will include timetables, information on who owns the data, and how the information will be stored and shared. You may also include when the metric will no longer be necessary.

By fully documenting the metric, it will make it well-defined, useful, and manageable. At a minimum, it should include the following:

- A purpose statement
- An explanation of how it will be used
- An explanation of how it won't be used
- A list of the customers of the metrics
- Schedules
- Analysis
- Visuals or "a picture for the rest of us"
- A narrative

The Purpose Statement

Is the purpose statement the same as your root question? The answer is, "maybe." You will document the purpose statement when you identify the root question as shown in Figure 3-2.

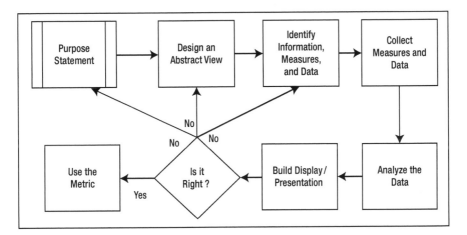

Figure 3-2. Purpose Statement

If you have a well-formed root question and you have dug as deep as you can, your root question may very well contain the purpose statement. Consider the following example:

Root Question: "How well are we providing customer support using online chat?"

Purpose Statement: "To ensure that we are providing world-class customer support using online chat."

Not much of a distinction between the two. It does provide a clearer requirement. It gives the underlying reasons for the question, and therefore the metric. The purpose of the metric is usually larger than providing insights or an answer to your root question. There is usually a central purpose to the question being asked. This purpose allows you to pull more than one metric together under an overarching requirement.

This underlying purpose will give us a much clearer guide for the metric. It will also allow us to identify other metrics needed, if you are ready to do so. You may have to settle for working with the question you currently have and get to the bigger-picture needs in the future. But it's always best to have the big picture—it allows you to keep the end in mind while working on parts of the picture.

Your root question is the foundation of the metric *and* the purpose statement. If you've identified a good root question, the question and your purpose may be one and the same.

When documenting the metric, I make a point to capture both the root question and the purpose. If they are synonymous, no harm is done. If they are not, then I gain more insight into what the metric is really all about.

Figure 3-3 shows the three major things to capture during the collection of data, measures and information.

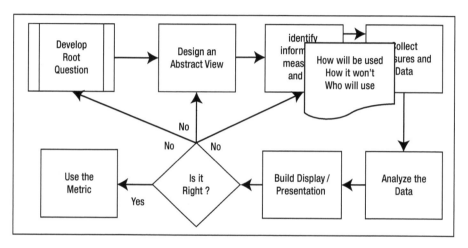

Figure 3-3. The "How" and "Who"

How Information Will Be Used

Along with the root question and purpose, you should articulate clearly *how the metric will be used*. This provides a key tool in helping overcome the fear people have of providing data. It will also help with the fear, uncertainty, and doubt people have toward the way the data will be used. Again, if you have a well-formed, clear, and foundational root question and purpose statement, this should be easy. While it may be easy to define how the metric will be used, that doesn't make the definition obvious. You need to ask the question directly: "How will you use the metric?" Your goal is to try and get the most direct answer. The more direct the question, the higher likelihood that you'll get a direct answer.

- *Vague answer:* "To improve our processes."

- *Direct answer:* "To measure how the changes we implemented affect the process."

- *More specific answer:* "To measure how the changes we implemented affect the process and allow for course corrections."

If public speaking is one of the greatest fears, the use of personal data might be a close second. Not just *any* numbers and values—but data that can be used to hurt an individual or create negative public perception of our organization. We imagine the worst, it's in our nature. So when we are asked to provide data, especially data that we believe reflects in any way upon ourselves or our departments, tremendous fear is created.

When we don't know the reason, we imagine the worst possible scenarios. It's our nature.

When the data you are collecting (and later analyzing and reporting on) can be indicators about an individual, the fear factor becomes exponentially greater. It doesn't even matter if you plan to use the data at an aggregate level, never looking at the individual. If the data *could* be used at the individual level, the fear is warranted.

Time to Resolve can be a good effectiveness measure, used to improve overall customer service. The purpose may be simply to achieve better customer service and, therefore, satisfaction. But if you fail to communicate this purpose, the root question, and how you will use the answers—the individuals providing the data will imagine the worst.

Be forewarned. Even if you have an automated system to collect the data (for example, the day and time the incident was opened and closed), the ones opening and closing the case in that system are still providing the data.

If the staff learns that you are gathering data on resolution speeds, they will "hear" that you are collecting data on how long it takes them to resolve the case. Not how long it takes the team or the organization to resolve most cases, but instead how long it takes each of them individually to do the work. And, if you are collecting data on an individual's performance, the individual in question will imagine all of the worst possible scenarios for how you will use that data.

So your innocent and proper Time to Resolve measure, if unexplained, could create morale problems due to fear, uncertainty, and doubt.

If fear is born of ignorance, then asking for data without sharing the purpose makes you the midwife.

We need to combat this common problem. To create a useful metric, you have to know, in advance of collecting the data, how the results (answers) will be used. It is essential for designing the metric properly and identifying the correct information, measures, and data. It is also essential if you want accurate data wherever human-provisioning is involved.

The explanation of how the metric and its components will be used should be documented. Don't get hung up on the need to make it pretty. Another key to getting better answers (or one at all if the respondent is still reluctant), is to communicate how the results *won't* be used.

Explain How Information *Won't* Be Used

If you want accurate data, you have to be able to assure the people involved in providing the data how you will and how you won't use the data. And how you *won't* use it may be more important to the person providing the data to you than how you *will* use it.

The most common and simple agreement I make is to not provide data to others without the source's permission. If you provide the data, it's your data. You should get to decide who sees it.

Defining how the metrics won't be used helps prevent fear, uncertainty, and doubt.

Identify Who Will Want to Use the Metrics

While you may believe you are the only customer who wants to view or use the metric, chances are there are many customers of your metrics. A simple test is to list all of the people you plan on sharing your information with. This list will probably include your boss, your workers, and those who use your service.

Anyone who will use your metric is a customer of it. You should only show it to customers.

Everyone that you plan to share your metrics with becomes a customer of that metric. If they are not customers, then there is no reason to share the information with them. You may be a proponent of openness and want to post your metrics on a public web site, but the information doesn't belong to you. It is the property of those providing the data. It is not public information; it was designed to help the organization answer a root question. Why share it with the world? And today we know that if you share it publicly, it's in the public domain forever.

The provider of the data should be the primary metric customer.

The possible customers are as follows:

- Those who provide the data that goes into creating the metric.
- Those who you choose to share your metrics with.
- Those who ask you for the metric *and* can clearly explain how they will use the metric.

It is important to clearly identify the customers of your metrics because they will have a say in how you present the metric, its validity, and how it will be used. If you are to keep to the promise of how it will and won't be used, you have to know who will use it and who won't.

Who will and won't use the metric is as important as how it will and won't be used.

Schedule for Reporting, Analyzing, and Collecting

The gathering of the data, measures, and information you will use to build the metric requires a simple plan. Figure 3-4 shows the timing for developing this part of the documentation.

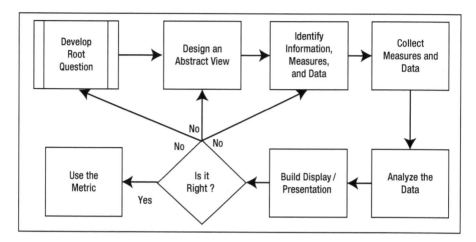

Figure 3-4. Schedules

Most metrics are time-based. You'll be looking at annual, monthly, or weekly reports of most metrics. Some are event-driven and require that you report them periodically. You will have to schedule at least three of the following facets of your metric:

- *Schedule for reporting.* Look at the schedule from the end backward to the beginning. Start with what you need. Take into account the customers that you've identified to help determine when you will need the metrics. Based on how the metrics will be used will also determine when you'll need to report it.

- *Schedule for analysis.* Based on the need, you can work backward to determine when you'll need to analyze the information to finalize the metric. This is the simplest part of the scheduling trifecta, since it is purely dependent upon how long it will take you to get the job done. Of course, the other variable is the amount of data and the complexity of the analysis. But, ultimately, you'll schedule the analysis far enough in advance to get it done and review your results.

- *Schedule for collection.* When will you collect the data? Based on when you will have to report the data, determine when you will need to analyze it. Then, based on that, figure out when you will need to collect it. Often, the schedule for collecting the data will be dependent on how you collect it. If it's automated, you may be able to gather it whenever you want. If it's dependent on human input, you may have to wait for periodic updates. If your data is survey-based, you'll have to wait until you administer the surveys and the additional time for people to complete them.

Since you started at the end, you know when you need the data and can work backwards to the date that you need to have the data in hand. Depending on the collection method you've chosen, you can plan out when you need to start the collection process and schedule accordingly.

If it's worth doing right, it's worth making sure you can do it right more than once. But remember, documenting the metric isn't just about repeatability, it's about getting it right the first time by forcing yourself to think it all out.

Analysis

Documenting analysis happens when you think it does. . .during the analysis phase.

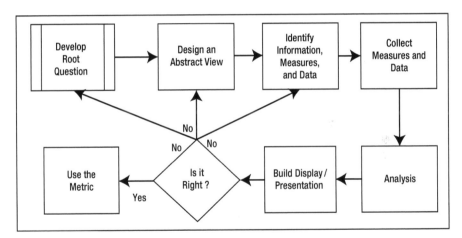

Figure 3-5. Analysis

After data collecting, the next thing most people think of when I mention metrics is analysis. All of the statistics classes I've taken lead to the same end: how to analyze the data you've carefully gathered. This analysis must include all metric data rules, edits, formulas, and algorithms; each should be clearly spelled out for future reference.

What may be in contention is the infallibility of the analysis tools. There are those that believe if you have accurate data (a few don't even care if it's accurate), you can predict, explain, or improve anything through statistical analysis. I'm not of that camp.

I have great respect for the benefits of analysis and, of course, I rely on it to determine the answers my metrics provide. For me, the design of the metric—from the root question, to the abstract picture, to the complete story—is more important than the analysis of the data. That may seem odd. If we fail to analyze properly, we will probably end up with the wrong conclusions and, thereby, the wrong answers. But, if we haven't designed the metric properly to begin with, we'll have no chance of the right answers—regardless of the quality of our analysis.

And if we have a good foundation (the right components), we should end up with a useful metric. If the analysis is off center, chances are we'll notice this in the reporting and review of the metric.

Without a strong foundation, the quality of the analysis is irrelevant.

While the analysis is secondary to the foundation, it is important to capture your analysis. The analysis techniques (formulas and processes) are the second-most volatile part of the metric (the first is the graphical representation). When the metric is reported and used, I expect it to be changed. If I've laid a strong foundation through my design, the final product will still need to be tweaked.

A Picture for the Rest of Us

You've drawn a picture of your metric. This picture was an abstract representation of the answer to the root question. Another major component of a well thought-out metric is another picture—one your customers can easily decipher. This picture is normally a chart, graph, or table. Plan to include one in your documentation.

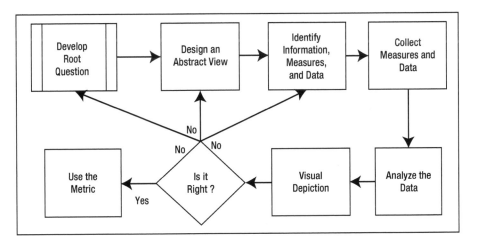

Figure 3-6. Visual Depiction

It can easily be more than one picture. If you need a dashboard made up of twelve charts, graphs, and tables—then so be it. If you've done a good job with the root question and abstract version of your metric, determining how you'll graphically represent the metric should be an easy step. If you pick a stacked bar chart, and later realize it should have been trend lines—you can change it. No harm done.

This component should be fun. Let your creativity shine through. Find ways to explain visually so that you need less prose. A picture can truly tell a story of a thousand words. No matter how good it is, you'll want to add prose to ensure the viewer gets it right, but we want that prose to be as brief as possible. We want the picture to tell the story, clearly. Don't over-complicate the picture.

You may, in fact, have more data than necessary to tell your story. You may find yourself reluctant to leave out information, but sometimes less really is more. Especially if the extra information could confuse the audience. You're not required to put data into your metric just because you've collected it.

Narrative Description

I love it when someone asks, "Do I have to spell it out for you?" My answer is frequently, "Thanks! That would be nice."

Why not? No matter how good your graphical representation is, you can't afford to risk a misunderstanding. You rooted out the question and you designed the metric so that you could provide the right answer to the right question. You cannot allow the viewer of the metric to misinterpret the story that you've worked so hard to tell.

The narrative is your chance to ensure the viewer sees what you see, the way you see it. They will hopefully hear what you are trying to tell them. Any part of the plan can be updated on a regular basis, but the narrative requires frequent documentation. Since the narrative explains what the metric is telling the viewer, the explanation has to change to match the story as it changes. The narration which accompanies the picture and documents what the metric means is critical to how the metric will be used.

Figure 3-7 shows when the narration is documented.

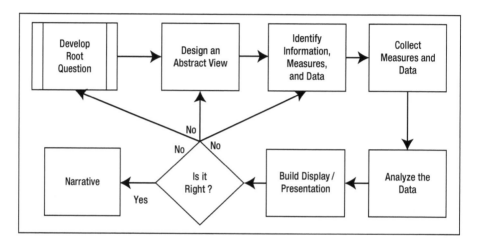

Figure 3-7. Narrative

Using the Documentation

It's valuable to put all of the details into one place. This will help you in the following three ways:

- It will help you think out the metric in a comprehensive manner.

- It will help you if you need to improve your processes.

- It will help you if you need to replicate the steps.

Figure 3-8 shows them all together in coordination with the process for developing the metric.

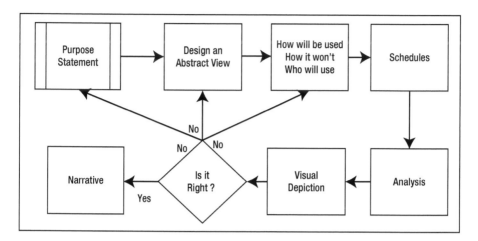

Figure 3-8. The Metric Development Process

Make the capture of your metric a living document. You will want it for reference and at times for evidence of agreements made. I find it extremely useful when the metrics are reported infrequently. The more infrequently the metrics are reported, the more likely I'll forget the steps I followed. The collection can be very complicated, cleaning the data can be complex, and the analysis can require even more detailed steps. The more complex and the more infrequent the process, the more likely I'll need the documentation.

Of course, even if I perform the process weekly, the responsible thing to do is to document it so others can carry it out in my absence. It provides a historical view as well as a "how to" guide. Without repeatability you can't improve.

Without repeatability, you can't improve.

When you document the components, don't be afraid to be verbose. This isn't a time for brevity. We need to build confidence in the metric and the components. We need to document as much information around each component as necessary to build trust in the following. To build that trust you have to pay special attention to:

- *Accuracy of the raw data.* You will be challenged on this, and rightfully so. People have their own expectations of what the answer to your root question should be. They will also have expectations regarding what the data should say about that question. Regardless of the answer, *someone* will think you have it wrong and check your data. Thus, you have to be accurate when you share the data. This requires that you perform quality checks of the data. It doesn't matter if the errors are due to your sources, your formulas, or a software glitch. If your data is proven to be wrong, your metrics won't be trusted or used.

Most examples of inaccurate raw data can be found as a result of human error but even automated tools are prone to errors, particularly in the interpretation of the data. When you're starting, there is nothing more important than accuracy of your raw data and the biggest risk to this accuracy comes when a human touches your data.

- *Accuracy of your analysis.* Anyone looking over your work should be able to replicate your work by hand (using pen, paper, and a calculator). This documentation is tedious but necessary. Your process must be repeatable. Your process *must* produce zero defects in the data, analysis, and results.

Without repeatability you don't really have a process.

How should you mitigate the inevitable mistakes you will undoubtedly make? Save early, save often, and save your work in more than one place. It won't hurt to have a hard copy of your work as a final safeguard. Along with backing up your data, it's important to have the processes documented.

You will make mistakes—it's inevitable. The key is to mitigate this reality as much as possible.

Another tool for mitigating mistakes is to use variables in all of your formulas. If you're using software to perform equations, avoid any raw data in the formulas. Put any values that you will reuse in a separate location (worksheet, table, or file). Not only does it allow you to avoid mistakes, it makes modifying the formulas easier.

Reference all values and keep raw data out of the equation.

Recap

I have introduced a taxonomy so that we can communicate clearly around the subject of metrics. In this chapter, I covered the theory and concept of designing a metric and the high-level process for collecting, analyzing, and reporting the data, measures, and information that go into making up that metric.

- *Getting to the root question*: It is imperative to get to the root question *before* you start even "thinking about" data. The root question will help you avoid waste. To get to the real root, I discussed using Five Whys, facilitating group interventions, and being willing to accept that the answer may not include metrics. Make sure you define every facet of the question so you are perfectly clear about what you want.

- *Testing the root question*: I provided some suggestions on how you can test if the question you've settled upon is a true root question. Even with the tests, it's important to realize that you may not have reached it when you draw your picture. You may have to do a little rework.

- *Developing a metric*: This is more about what you shouldn't do than what you should. You shouldn't think about data. You shouldn't design charts and graphs. You shouldn't jump to what measures you want. Stay abstract.

- *Being an artist*: The best way I've found to stay abstract is to be creative. The best way to be creative is to avoid the details and focus on the big picture. One helps feed the other. Draw a picture—it doesn't have to be a work of art.

- *Identifying the information, measures, and data needed*: Once you have a clear picture (literally and figuratively) it's time to think about information, measures and data. Think of it like a paint-by-numbers picture. What information is required to fill the picture in? What color paints will you need? And make sure you don't leave out any essential components.

- *Collecting measures and data*: Now that you know what you need, how do you collect it?

- *How to collect data*: I presented four major methods for collecting data: Using *automated sources, employing software and hardware, conducting surveys, and using people.*

I also covered the basics of how and where to document your work. The metric is made up of the following components you need to document:

- A purpose statement
- An explanation of how it will be used
- An explanation of how it won't be used
- A list of the customers of the metrics
- Schedules
- Analysis
- Visuals or "a picture for the rest of us"
- A narrative

Accuracy is critical. I stressed the importance of accuracy in your data (source dependent), your collection (process dependent) and your analysis (process and tool dependent). I also offered the benefits of making your processes repeatable.

Using Metrics as Indicators

To keep things simple, thus far I've focused only on the following basic concepts:

- Metrics are made up of basic components: data, measures, information, and other metrics.

- Metrics should be built from a root question.

- It's more important to share how you won't use a metric than how you will.

This chapter introduces another basic concept about creating and using metrics—metrics are nothing more than indicators. That may seem to be a way of saying they aren't powerful, but we know that's not the case. Metrics can be extremely powerful. Rather, the concept of metrics as indicators warns us not to elevate metrics to the status of truth.

Metrics' considerable power is proven by how much damage they can do. Metrics' worth is rooted in their inherent ability to ignite conversations. Metrics should lead to discussions between customers and service providers, between management and staff. Conversations should blossom around improvement opportunities and anomalies in the data. The basis for these conversations should be the investigation, analysis, and resolution of indicators provided through metrics.

Metrics should be a catalyst to investigation, discussion, and only then, action. The only proper response to metrics is to investigate—a directed and focused investigation into the truth behind the indicator.

Facts Aren't Always True

If you search the internet for things we know to be true (supported, of course, by data), you'll eventually find more than one site that offers evidence "debunking" past and present-day myths. What was thought to be a fact is proven to be an incorrect application of theory or the misinterpretation of data.

Health information is a ripe area, full of things people once believed to be true but now believe the opposite. Think about foods that were considered good for you ten years ago but today are not. Or foods that were considered not to be good for you, which now are considered healthy fare. Are eggs good for you or not? The answer not only depends on who you ask, but when.

- The US Government's "food pyramid" changes periodically.

- Who doesn't remember the scenes of Rocky downing raw eggs?

- It seems like each year we get a new "diet" to follow— high protein, high cholesterol, low fat, no red meat, or fish…the arguments change regularly.

One good argument on the topic of old facts not being in line with new truths is that facts don't change, just our interpretation of them.

This misrepresentation of metrics as fact can be seen in instances where only a portion of the metric is relayed to the viewer.

A business example is one a friend of mine loves to tell about the service desk analyst who was by all accounts taking three to five times as long to close cases as the other analysts. The "fact" was clear—he was less efficient. He was closing less than half of the cases as his peers and taking much longer to close each case. His "numbers" were abysmal.

The manager of the service desk took this "fact" and made a decision. It may not have helped his thought process that this "slow" worker was also the oldest and had been on the service desk longer than any of the analysts. The manager at the time made the mistake of believing the data he was looking at was a "fact" rather than an indicator. And rather than investigate the matter, he took immediate action.

> He called the weak performer into his office and began chewing him out. When he finally finished his critique he gave the worker a chance to speak, if only to answer this question (veiled threat): "So, what are you going to do about this? How are you going to improve your time to resolve cases? I want to see you closing more cases, faster."
>
> Showing a great deal more patience than he felt at the moment, the worker replied, "My first question is, how is the quality of my work?"

"Lousy! I just told you. You're the slowest analyst on the floor!"

"That's only how fast I work, not how good the quality is. Are you getting any complaints?"

"Well, no."

"Any complaints from customers?"

"No."

"How about my coworkers? Any complaints from them?"

"No," said the manager. "But the data doesn't lie."

"You're right, it doesn't lie. It's just not telling the whole story and therefore it isn't the truth."

"What? Are you trying to tell me you aren't the slowest? You are the one who closes the cases. Are you just incompetent?" The manager was implying that he wasn't closing the cases when done.

"No, I am the slowest," admitted the worker. "And no, I'm not incompetent, just the opposite. Have you asked anyone on the floor why I'm slow?"

"No—I'm asking you."

"Actually you never asked me why. You started out by showing me data that shows that I'm 'slow, inefficient,' and now 'incompetent.'"

The manager wasn't happy with the turn this had taken. The employee continued, "Did you check the types of cases I'm closing? I'm actually faster than most of my coworkers. If you looked at how fast I close simple cases, you'd see that I'm one of the fastest."

"The data doesn't break out that way," said the manager. "How am I supposed to know the types of cases each of you close?"

The employee replied, "Ask?" He was silent a moment. "If you had asked me or anyone else on the floor why I take longer to close cases and why I close fewer cases you'd find out a few things. I close fewer cases because I take longer to close my cases. The other analysts give me any cases that they can't resolve. I get the hardest cases to close because I have the most experience. I am not slow, inefficient, or incompetent. Just the opposite. I'm the best analyst you have on the floor."

The manager looked uncomfortable.

The employee continued, "So, tell me, what do you want me to change? If you want, I won't take any cases from the other analysts and I'll let the customers' toughest problems go unresolved. Your call. You're the boss."

Needless (but fun) to say, the boss never bothered him about his time to resolve again. And luckily for all involved, the boss did not remain in the position much longer.

The only proper initial response to metrics is to investigate.

Metrics are not facts, treating them as such over values them. This is dangerous when leadership decides to "drive" decisions with metrics. When we elevate metrics to truth, we stop looking deeper. We also risk making decisions and taking actions based on information that may easily be less than 100 percent accurate.

Metrics are not facts. They are indicators.

When we give metrics an undeserved lofty status (as truth instead of indicators) we encourage our organization to "chase data" rather than work toward the underlying root question the metrics were designed to answer. We send a totally clear and equally wrong message to our staff that the metrics are what matter. We end up trying to influence behavior with numbers, percentages, charts, and graphs.

One of the major benefits of building a metric the way I suggest is that it tells a complete story in answer to a root question. If you've built it well, chances are, it's accurate and comprehensive. It is the closest thing you'll get to the truth. But, I know from experience, no matter how hard I try there is always room for error and misinterpretation. A little pause for the cause of investigation won't hurt—and it may help immensely.

Metrics Can Be Wrong

Since there is the possibility of variance and error in any collection method, there is always room for doubting the total validity of any measure. If you don't have a healthy skepticism of what the information says, you will be led down the wrong path as often as not. Let's say the check-engine light in your car comes on. Let's also say that the car is new. Even if we know that the light is a malfunction indicator, we should refrain from jumping to conclusions. My favorite visits to the mechanics are when they run their diagnostics on my check-engine light and they determine that the only problem *is* with the check-engine light.

Perhaps you are thinking that the fuel-level indicator would be a better example. If the fuel gauge reads near empty, especially if the warning light accompanies it, you can have a high level of confidence that you need gas. But the gas gauge is still only an indicator. Perhaps it's a more reliable one than the check-engine light, but it's still only an indicator. Besides the variance involved (I noticed that when on a hill the gauge goes from nearly empty to nearly an eighth of a tank!), there is still the possibility of a stuck or broken gauge.

I understand if you choose to believe the gas gauge, the thermometer, or the digital clock—which are single measures. But, when you're looking at metrics, which are made up of multiple data, measures, and information, I hope you do so with a healthy dose of humility toward your ability to interpret the meaning of the metric.

This healthy humility keeps us from rushing to conclusions or decisions based solely on indicators (metrics).

I've heard (too often for my taste) that metrics should "drive" decisions. I much prefer the attitude and belief that metrics should "inform" decisions.

Accurate Metrics Are Still Simply Indicators

Putting aside the possibility of erroneous data, there are important reasons to refrain from putting too much trust in metrics.

Let's look at an example from the world of Major League Baseball. I like to use baseball because of all the major sports, baseball is easily the most statistically focused. Fans, writers, announcers, and players alike use statistics to discuss America's pastime. It is arguably an intrinsic part of the game.

To be in the National Baseball Hall of Fame is, in many ways, the pinnacle of a player's career. Let's look at one of the greatest player's statistics. In 2011, I was able to witness Derek Jeter's 3,000th hit (a home run), one of the accomplishments a player can achieve to essentially assure his position in the Hall of Fame (Jeter was only the 28th player of all time to achieve this). The question was immediately raised—could Jeter become the all-time leader in hits? The present all-time leader had 4,256 hits! Personally, I don't think Jeter will make it.

The all-time hits leader was also voted as an All-Star 17 times in a 23-year career—at an unheard of five different positions. He won three World Series championships, two Golden Glove Awards, one National League Most Valuable Player (MVP) award, and also a World Series MVP award. He also won Rookie of the Year and the Lou Gehrig Memorial Award and was selected to Major League Baseball's All-Century Team. According to one online source, his MLB records are as follows:

- Most hits
- Most outs
- Most games played
- Most at bats
- Most singles
- Most runs by a switch hitter
- Most doubles by a switch hitter
- Most walks by a switch hitter
- Most total bases by a switch hitter
- Most seasons with 200 or more hits
- Most consecutive seasons with 100 or more hits
- Most consecutive seasons with 600 at bats
- Only player to play more than 500 games at each of five different positions

This baseball player holds a few other world records, as well as numerous National League records that include most runs and doubles.

In every list I could find, he was ranked in the top 50 of all-time baseball players. In 1998 *The Sporting News* ranked him as the 25th and The Society for American Baseball Research placed him at 48th.

So, based on all of this objective, critically checked data, it should be easily understood why this professional baseball player was unanimously elected to the National Baseball Hall of Fame on the first ballot that he was eligible for.

But he wasn't elected.

His name is Pete Rose. He is not in the Baseball Hall of Fame and may never get there. If you look at all of the statistical data that the voters for the Hall use, his selection is a no-brainer. But the statistics, while telling a complete story, lack the input that was taken into account—specifically that he broke one of baseball's not-to-be-breached rules: he legally and illegally gambled on professional baseball games.

In the face of the overwhelming "facts" that Pete Rose should be in the Baseball Hall of Fame, the truth is in direct contrast to the data.

Even if we look at well-defined metrics that tell a full story, they are only indicators in the truest sense. If you fully and clearly explain the results of your investigation, you complete the metric by explaining the meaning of the indicator. You explain what the metrics indicate so that better decisions can be made, improvement opportunities identified, or progress determined. You are providing an interpretation—hopefully one backed by the results of your investigation.

No matter how you decorate it, metrics are only indicators and as such should elicit only one initial response: to investigate.

Indicators: Qualitative vs. Quantitative Data

The simple difference between qualitative and quantitative data is that qualitative data is made up of opinions and quantitative data is made up of objective numbers. Qualitative data is more readily accepted to be an indicator, while quantitative data is more likely to be mistakenly viewed as fact, without any further investigation necessary. Let's look at these two main categories of indicators.

Qualitative Data

Customer satisfaction ratings are opinions—a qualitative measure of how satisfied your customer is. Most qualitative collection tools consist of surveys and interviews. They can be in the form of open-ended questions, multiple-choice questions, or ratings. Even observations can be qualitative, if they don't involve capturing "numbers"—like counting the number of strikes in baseball, or the number of questions about a specific product line. When observations capture the opinions of the observer, we still have qualitative data.

Many times, qualitative data is what is called for to provide answers to our root question. Besides asking how satisfied your customers are, some other examples are:

- How satisfied are your workers?
- Which product do your customers prefer, regular or diet?
- How fast do they want it?
- How much money are your customers willing to pay?
- When do your customers expect your service to be available?
- Do your workers feel appreciated?

No matter how you collect this data, they are opinions. They are not objective data. They are not, for the most part, even numbers.

Some analysts, especially those that believe the customer is always right, believe that qualitative data is the best data. Through open-ended questions these analysts believe you receive valuable feedback on your processes, products, and services. Since the customer is king, what better analytical tool is there than to capture the customers' opinion on your products and services?

But is a survey response truly the respondent's opinion?

Someone could rate your product high or low on a satisfaction scale for many reasons other than the product's quality. Some factors that could go into a qualitative evaluation of your service or product could include:

- The time of day the question was asked
- The mood the respondent was in before you asked the question
- Past experiences of the respondent with similar products or services
- The temperature of the room
- The lighting
- The attractiveness of the person asking the question
- If the interviewer has a foreign accent

The list can go on forever. The problem is that these results are not facts. They are still only opinions, and in most cases there is low confidence that respondents even provide their actual opinion.

Quantitative Data

Quantitative data usually means numbers—objective measures without emotion. This includes all of the gauges in your car. They also include information from automated systems like automated-call tools, which tell you how many calls were answered, how long it took for them to be answered, and how long the call lasted.

The debate used to be that one form of data was better than another. It was argued that quantitative data was better because it avoided the natural inconsistencies of data based on emotional opinions.

Quantitative data avoids the variances we saw with qualitative data and gets directly to the things that can be counted. Some examples in the customer satisfaction scenario could include:

- The number of customers who bought your product
- The number of times a customer buys the product
- The amount of money the customer paid for your product
- What other products the customer bought
- The number of product returns

The proponents of quantitative information would argue that this is much more reliable and, therefore, more meaningful data.

I'm sure you've guessed that neither camp is entirely correct. I'm going to suggest using a mix of both types of data.

Quantitative and Qualitative Data

For the most part, the flaws with qualitative data can be best alleviated by including some quantitative data—and vice versa. Qualitative data, when taken in isolation, is hard to trust because of the many factors that can lead to the information you collect. If a customer says that they love your product or service, but never buy it, the warm fuzzy you receive from the positive feedback will not help when the company goes out of business. Quantitative data on the number of sales and repeat customers can help provide faith in the qualitative feedback.

If we look at quantitative data by itself, we risk making some unwise decisions. If our entire inventory of a test product sells out in one day, we may decide that it is a hot item and we should expect to sell many more. Without qualitative data to support this assumption, we may go into mass production and invest large sums. Qualitative questions could have informed us of why the item sold out so fast. We may learn that the causes for the immediate success were unlikely to recur and therefore we may need to do more research and development before going full speed ahead. Perhaps the product sold out because a confused customer was sent to the store to buy a lot of product X and instead bought a lot of your product by mistake. Perhaps it sold quickly because it was a new product with a novel look, but when asked, the customers assured you they'd not buy it again—that they didn't like it.

Not only should you use both types of data (and the accompanying data collection methods), but you should also look to collect more than one of each. And of course, once you do, you have to investigate the results.

Even in the case of automated-call software, the results are only indicators.

Quantitative data, while objective, are still only indicators. If you don't know why the numbers are what they are, you will end up guessing at the reasons behind the numbers. If you guess at the causes, you are guessing at the answer.

Metrics (indicators) require interpretation to be used properly.

The great debate between which is better is unnecessary. You should use some of each in your recipe.

Recap

The following are principles to remember:

- *Metrics are only indicators.*

- Metrics are not facts. Even when you have a high level of confidence in their accuracy, don't elevate them to the status of truth.

- The only proper response to a metric is to investigate.

- When you tell the story by adding prose, you are explaining what the metrics are indicating so that better decisions can be made, or improvement opportunities identified, or progress determined.

- There are two main categories of indicators: Qualitative and Quantitative. Qualitative is subjective in nature and usually an expression of opinion. Quantitative is objective in nature and compiled using automated, impartial tools.

- Metrics by themselves don't provide the answers; they help us ask the right questions and take the right actions.

- *Metrics require interpretation to be useful.*

- *Even the interpretation is open to interpretation—metrics aren't about providing truth, they're about providing insight.*

Using the Answer Key

A Shortcut

The Answer Key is a tool for helping ensure you have the right answer to your root question. It works with the majority of organizational improvement questions. It will also give you ideas about other areas you may want to measure. You'll get the most benefit when you use the Answer Key to work on organizational improvement efforts.

What Is the Answer Key?

The Answer Key can be used when your root question concerns the health of the organization. This covers a wide range of questions and needs we usually develop metrics for. Most root questions, especially in a business, revolve around how well the organization is functioning. Most Balanced Scorecards and questions about customer satisfaction fit under this umbrella.

The Answer Key is a shortcut for many of the metrics you'll encounter. It includes the metrics I recommend organizations start with when they are seeking to implement a metrics program for the first time.

The Answer Key helps you determine where you need to go with your metrics. It also identifies other questions that may relate to the one you're starting with. It can also help you keep from going in the wrong direction and dispersing your efforts too broadly, with no focus.

The Answer Key is made up of tiers that branch out from left to right. Each tier has more measures and data than the previous tier. The following sections will describe each of these tiers in more detail.

Answer Key: First Tier

The first tier isn't so much of a tier as it is a starting point. Is your root question an organizational information need? Does your root question deal with information about an organization; specifically, about the health of the organization? If so, your question will probably fall under one of the following two concerns:

- How well you provide services and products to your customers

- How healthy the future looks for your organization

Answer Key: Second Tier

If your root question fits within one of the first two tiers of the Answer Key, this tool will help you focus your efforts and find viable measures without spending inordinate amounts of time hunting for them. But, if your question does not fit into the Answer Key, don't change your question so you can use this shortcut!

Also don't ignore the need for developing the root question first. In other words, don't start with the key. If you do, you'll end up short-circuiting your efforts to develop useful metrics and more importantly, to answer your questions.

Tier two provides a framework for strategic-level root questions. If your root question is at the vision level, the second tier may represent actual metrics. When you find your root question is based on improving the organization, the question is often based on a need to understand "where the organization is" and "where it is going." The Answer Key shows that this need for information flows into two channels, one to show the return (what we get) vs. our investment (what we put in) and the other to assist in the management of resources. I call these two branches "Return vs. Investment" and "The State of the Union." Figure 5-1 shows this branching.

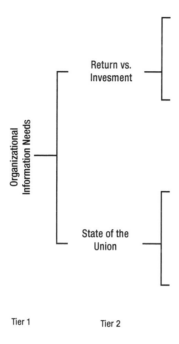

Figure 5-1. The Answer Key, tiers one and two

Return vs. Investment

Return vs. Investment is the first of the two main branches of organizational metrics. It represents the information needed to answer questions concerning how well the organization is functioning and how well it is run. Are we doing the right things? Are we doing the right things the right way? These are key focus areas for improvement and, actually, for survival. If you aren't doing the "right" things, chances are you will soon be out of business or, at the least, out of a job.

If you aren't doing things the right way, you may find that you can continue to function and the business may continue to survive, but any meaningful improvement is highly unlikely. The best you will be able to hope for is to survive, but not thrive.

Root questions around the *return* may include

- How well are we providing our key services?
- In what ways can we improve our key services?

Questions around the *investment* may include

- How much does it cost us to provide our key services?

- How well are we managing our resources?

The breadth of your root question will determine how far to the left you'll need to go. The farther left on the Answer Key, the more broad or strategic the question.

State of the Union

Once you are effectively and efficiently running the business, you can turn your attention to how you manage your resources. The most valuable assets you have should be maintained with loving care. Yes, I'm talking about your workforce. Every boss I've ever had has touted the same mantra: "Our most valuable assets are our people." Yet it's amazing to me how poorly we take care of those admittedly invaluable assets.

I observe managers who take their BMWs to their dealers for scheduled maintenance, only use premium gasoline (regardless of the price of gas), and won't park anywhere near another car—yet do absolutely nothing to maintain their workforce. No training plans, no employee satisfaction surveys, not even a suggestion program. They rarely listen to their staff and devalue them by never asking for input. If people are truly our greatest assets, then we should treat them as such.

This view of the organization tells us how healthy our organization is internally. While Return vs. Investment tells us how healthy the organization is from a customer and business point of view, the State of the Union tells us how healthy the culture is.

Besides the workforce, we also need to focus on the potential for our future. We can determine this by looking at how we are managing our growth toward maturity. Do we have good strategic plans for our future? Are we working toward our goals?

Root questions you may encounter in this area include the following:

- How strong is the culture of recognition in our organization?

- How strong is the loyalty of our workforce?

- How well are our professional-development efforts working?

- What is the expected future of our organization?

- How do we stack up against our competition?

- How well are we achieving our strategic goals?

The further to the right you move on the Answer Key, the more specific and tactical your root questions will become.

Answer Key: Third Tier

Figure 5-2 shows the next level of the Answer Key, in which we extend the branches to include Product/Service Health (effectiveness), Process Health (efficiency), Organizational Health (employee maintenance), and Future Health (projects and strategic planning).

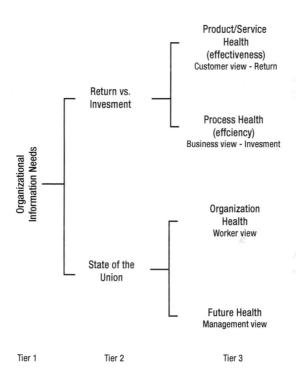

Figure 5-2. The Answer Key, tiers one, two, and three

Most root questions boil down to wanting to know answers based on one of the views of the organization represented in the third tier. The titles—Product/Service Health, Process Health, Organizational Health, and Future Health—help us to understand the relationship of each branch to the other. They also help us understand where our metric fits. Along with the titles, we find an accompanying viewpoint to further assist in reading the Answer Key. These viewpoints show that each of the titles can be looked at from the perspective of Customers, the Business, the Workers, and finally Management.

Let's figure out where your root question best fits.

Does your root question deal with how well you provide a service or product? Does it ask if you are doing the right things? Does it ask if the things you are doing satisfy the needs or desires of your customers? Is your root question one the customer would ask? If your question matches any of these, it fits into the Product/Service Health category.

Does your root question touch on how well you perform the processes necessary to deliver the services or products? How efficient you are? How long it takes or how much it costs for you to perform the tasks in the process? Is your question one a frontline manager would ask? If your question can be found in any of these, you are probably looking at a Process Health root question.

If your root question concerns human resources, the staff, or something a compassionate leader would ask, your question may belong in the Organizational Health branch. Root questions here ask about the morale of the workforce, loyalty, and retention rates for employees, among other things. How well do you treat your staff? Is your organization among the top 100 places to work in your industry?

The final area of the third tier represents root questions that are concerned with the Future Health of the organization. Is the organization suffering from organizational immaturity? How useful are the strategic plans, mission statement, and vision of the organization? How well is research and development progressing? This view is primarily one of top leadership—if your leadership and the organization are ready to look ahead.

How would you use the Answer Key to develop your metrics?

The information needed to define the Return vs. Investment is made up of the well-trod paths of "effectiveness" and "efficiency." Effectiveness is the organization's health from the customer's point of view. How well is the organization delivering on its promises? Is the organization doing the right things? This is not only important for the development of viable metrics, but for understanding and growing the culture of the organization. Some organizations may not even know who its customers are. And if the customer base has been well defined, gathering the customer's view of the components of effectiveness is not seen as important.

Sometimes organizations are forced to ask customers what they think of the company's effectiveness. Surveys are built, focus groups are formed, and the questions are asked.

- Do you use our products or services?
- Are you satisfied with the delivery of our products and services?
- How satisfied are you with our organization?

While these questions help define viable measures, they also give focus for your own growth. Does the organization have a clearly-defined and documented list of customers? Does the organization know what its products and services are? Is the organization in the business of satisfying the customer? How does the organization "serve" the customer? These are more than guidelines for gathering data points. The Answer Key helps form a picture for an organization seeking to achieve continuous improvement.

While these four sections can describe the metrics themselves (if you have a higher-level root question), chances are your root question is at this level and your metrics won't start until the fourth tier.

Answer Key: Fourth Tier

Now we'll look at the level most organizations start and finish with. When your root question starts here, you have tactical, low-level questions. This is to be expected when an organization is first starting to use metrics. The root questions you'll encounter will be very specific and may only address a small area. You may have a root question about delivery that asks, "How well are we responding to customers' requests for updates?" for example.

You may have root questions around specific Process Health issues, like the amount of time it takes to produce a widget, the quality of your output, or the cost for a specific service. Where your root question falls in the Answer Key changes the character of each tier. Figure 5-3 introduces the fourth tier.

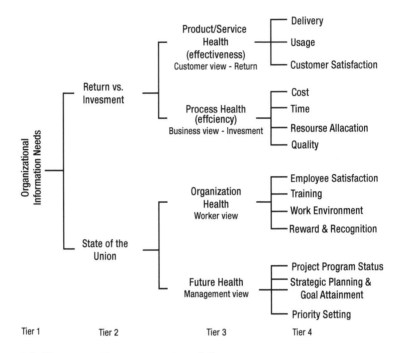

Figure 5-3. The Answer Key, tiers one through four

If your root question comes out of the fourth tier, everything to the left is context for the question. As your organization matures, you'll move your questions to the left, asking questions from a more strategic position. If your root question were in tier two, then tier three would represent the metrics you could use and tier four would represent information. The measures and data would be defined for each information set—and could become a fifth and sixth tier if necessary.

The Answer Key not only keeps you focused and helps you determine what area you're interested in; it also provides some standard metrics, information, and measures, depending on where your root question falls.

Product/Service Health (effectiveness)

The following are the main components of Product/Service Health (Figure 5-4):

- *Delivery*: How well are you delivering your products and/or services?

- *Usage*: Are your products and/or services being used?

- *Customer satisfaction*: What do your customers think of your products and/or services?

Figure 5-4. The Answer Key, Quadrant 1, Product/Service Health

Each component can be broken down into smaller bits—making it more palatable. Delivery is a good example for this as it is a higher-level concept. I tend to break delivery into the following parts:

- *Availability*: Is the service/product available when the customer wants it?

- *Speed*: How long does it take to deliver the service/product?

- *Accuracy*: Do we deliver what we say we will or are there errors involved?

The driving force behind Product/Service Health is the customer. We don't care who is "responsible" for the issue. We don't care if you have any control over the situation or condition. All we're trying to see is how the customer views our products and services. This simplistic way of looking at your organization is valuable because it makes it easy to focus on what is most important.

Process Health (efficiency)

The other component of Return vs. Investment is efficiency, or is the organization doing things the "right way?" This (Figure 5-5) captures a business view that all stakeholders should want to claim. The following, tested components of efficiency remain relevant:

- *Cost*: What is the cost-benefit of the way we perform our processes?

- *Time*: Time is akin to speed in the customer view. Many times the same data and sources can be reused for this measure. How much time does it take to perform a task or process?

- *Resource allocation*: How efficiently do we distribute the work? Do we assign work by type and amount?

- *Quality*: Quality is accuracy from the business point of view. Even if we have redundant systems providing 100 percent uptime, we will need to track that reliability (for each of those systems) so that we can best maintain them.

Figure 5-5. The Answer Key, Quadrant 2, Process Health

Many organizations focus too much on cost and forget that their concerns should first be based around whether the organization is doing the right things (effectiveness) and only then if it is doing them the right way (efficiency). Instead, many organizations latch onto any perceived faults in cost and then react without deep or critical thought. This error is compounded by the lack of information about the costs of services and production. This is especially noticeable in the soft industries. Manufacturing usually has a good handle on cost data, but soft industries like information technology, software development, or education find it very difficult to price out their products and services. This is logical, since these organizations normally have trouble defining what products and services they produce. Ask a dean of a given college what products and services the organization delivers. Then take a step further and see if the cost of those offerings is documented.

Time, especially when it is connected to cost as a delimiter (person/hours), is one of the most abused pieces of information. Managers jump on the metrics bandwagon when they start to believe that they can ask for data that will allow them to manage (not coach or lead) their people without having to actually talk to them or get to know them. Timesheets, time-motion studies, and time allocation worksheets come to be in vogue. In a well-constructed metrics program, you wouldn't get to this level without starting from the all-important root and all of its listed components, which should prevent one from abusing the data. Time shouldn't be used to "control" your workforce. It should be used to do the following:

- Improve the organization's ability to estimate delivery schedules

- Assist in improving process and procedures

- Round out other data, like cost and quality

If "quality" is based on the objective measure of defects, how many defects per a thousand instances equals "quality?" Is high quality the goal? Is quality a "yes or no" decision? Quality is best described in terms of defects and rework, and like "time" it can be misused. It is not a simple way for managers to determine who should get a raise or any other human resources issue. If you abuse metrics, *quality can become a weapon instead of a tool.*

Ensure your metrics are used as a tool for improvement and not a weapon.

Quality, time, resource allocation, and cost are all components of Process Health and define the business view of the Investment the organization's processes and procedures represent. Therefore, these views should only be used to improve the business—not people. Product/Service Health was exclusively from the customers' viewpoint. Process Health is equally exclusive in its focus—and it represents the business view. The customer will most likely never see (and shouldn't have a need to see) these metrics. These are "internal" metrics, as are the next two areas of the fourth tier.

Metrics should be used to improve the overall business, not people.

Organizational Health

When we look at Organizational Health (Figure 5-6), we look at the organization from the worker's viewpoint. It takes into account the following:

- Employee satisfaction

- Professional development

- Work environment

- Reward and recognition

Figure 5-6. The Answer Key, Quadrant 3, Organizational Health

When we ensure that our most valuable assets are treated as such, we find that the organization improves. I normally suggest organizations address the Answer Key areas from the top down, making the Organizational Health measures third or fourth. This is in part due to political concerns. When you justify the use of metrics, it's much easier to gain support if you first address the organization's health from the customers' point of view. Without customers, there won't be a business to improve. Once you've tackled the customer's view, you will need to ensure that you can afford to keep your workforce.

But in an ideal world, one in which perhaps you are the CEO, I'd argue easily that the first place to start your improvement efforts should be with your greatest assets, and then with your customers. Sound blasphemous? If you have a healthy workforce, you can work with them to better define your business model, your future, and where you want to improve.

Employee satisfaction is pretty straightforward. The more satisfied your workforce is with their situation, the organization, and the environment, the harder they will work. The more loyal they will be. The stronger your organization will become.

Along with their satisfaction, you must be concerned with developing their skills and their knowledge base. Professional development measures tell you how well you're doing in this area. Do you have training plans for each worker? What is the level of skill development for each worker? The stronger your workforce, the more you'll be able to do. It should be a criminal offense to first eliminate training whenever funding cuts come down. The only way to do more with less is to increase the capacity of our workforce to produce more and produce better. The best way to improve productivity is to improve the worker's skill set.

The work environment measures are normally captured through subjective tools—like surveys. But there are plenty of objective measures available. Square footage for workspace. Air quality. Lighting. Ergonomics. There are many ways to measure the quality of the physical work environment. There is also the cultural work environment. Is the organization a pleasant place to work? Is it a high stress environment (and if it is, does it need to be)? Again, you can find both subjective (ask the workers) and objective measures. Do workers take a lot of vacation and sick time? Is turnover high?

The final component of Organizational Health is reward and recognition. The simple questions may not require data collection. Do you have a formal reward or recognition program? Is it effective? Does it do what you want it to? How do you reward your workers? How do you recognize their accomplishments? Do you only recognize their work-related achievements? And on a more subtle note, do you inadvertently combine recognition and reward, such that recognition only occurs when there is a reward involved?

The bottom line on Organizational Health is an extremely easy one—do you treat your most valuable asset like they are your most valued asset?

Future Health

The last area of the Answer Key is Future Health (Figure 5-7). It covers the following:

- Project/Program status

- Strategic planning: How well the organization is implementing the strategic plan

- Goal attainment: How well the organization is reaching its goals

- Priority setting: How well priorities are being set, and being met

Figure 5-7. The Answer Key, Quadrant 4, Future Health

This area assumes that you are working on continuous improvement for the organization. Future Health is not listed last because it isn't as important as the others. It's last in the list because most organizations are not ready for attempting metrics in this area. Most organizations need to get the first three areas of the fourth tier under control before they start to look at large-scale improvement efforts.

Many organizations bypass this guidance and jump to measures to show how well they are working to improve processes. They jump on the continuous process improvement wagon. I don't put much faith in such behaviors since these organizations drop these same efforts as soon as funding becomes tight.

The reason you undertake an improvement effort is more important than if you succeed at it. The only way you can truly succeed is to do the right things for the right reasons.

Measures around the organization's Future Health are mostly predictive, and this makes them "sexy" to leadership. But more important than predicting the future is encouraging and rewarding true process improvement.

Program and project status measures provide insights for leadership into how these efforts are helping improve the organization. You should expect that progress in process improvement is or will be reflected in the measures captured in the other three areas. If you do a good job on continuous process improvement, the customer view should improve. The business view should also see gains, and the workforce should also benefit. If these three areas aren't improved by your efforts, you aren't improving the organization.

Strategic planning, goal attainment, and priority setting are all important things to focus on—but in themselves they are meaningless. If these are not part of a bigger effort to improve the organization, you are just spinning your wheels. These efforts are tough because they require true (and sometimes reckless) commitment to succeeding. You have to want to change. Many organizations pay lip service to this area and don't really see the effort through to the end—and when we're talking about "continuous" process improvement—there really isn't an end.

Answer Key: The Fifth Tier and Beyond

The fifth tier would introduce specific measures for each of the "information" within each of the viewpoints presented. While your root question could conceivably be here, it is unlikely. If you find your question starts here, you probably don't have a need for a metric. Instead, you probably only need a measure.

The elements you're most likely to find here are measures. For example, extending from the top branch of Usage in the fourth tier you may find the following branching out into a fifth tier:

- Unique customers by month, by type

- Number of purchases, by type

- Number of repeat customers

It is unnecessary to list possible measures for each of the fourth tier's elements. It won't make any sense to try to list each of what would be in tier six or seven—lower-level measures or data. In the examples for Usage, we might see data points as follows:

- Number of customers

- Names of each customer

- Products listed by type

- Dates and times of each purchase

How to Use the Answer Key: Identify Types of Measures

The Answer Key can be used to identify measures you can use to answer your root question. If you have done your homework and defined the root question and developed your abstract design, you are now ready for the next step—identifying possible measures to fill out the metric.

The Answer Key can help with this phase of the process. Take your root question and metric design and determine where you are on the Answer Key. If your question deals with the value of the organization, then you're on the top tier, Return vs. Investment. If your question is in the realm of managing organizational resources, you're on the lower tier, State of the Union.

We used some examples of root questions earlier. One was based on the distribution of work. This would fit under the fourth tier, Process Health–Resource Allocation. Using this tool, we not only can identify the type of measures we'll need, but we understand the area of focus of our question. Moving to the left from Resource Allocation, we can see that our question is dealing with the business view (investment). If our question is a root question, we can use the Five Whys. And now we can also ask if our concerns are bigger than just Resource Allocation (measure centered). Are our concerns actually around Process Health? Are we missing the measures around cost, time, and quality?

If your root question is answered by just one of the measures in the fourth tier, chances are you don't have the root question. You definitely don't have a metric.

Using the Answer Key allows us to do a quick and easy quality check on the measures we've identified. For example, if the metric is a Worker view (based on the root question), and you find some of the measures you identified are from the Customer view (like delivery measures), then either those measures are wrong for the metric, or, possibly your metric is not the right one for answering the question. As a general rule, I find that the measures are usually misplaced, rather than that the metric is incorrect.

On Triangulation

Using the concept of triangulation is essential to creating effective metrics. I bow to Norman K. Denzin, a professor of communications and sociology at the University of Illinois at Urbana-Champaign, for his using "triangulation" to mean using more than two methods to collect data in the context of gathering and using research data. My definition is much like it—using multiple measures, as well as collection methods, for processing the information used in a metric.

A major reason for using triangulation, according to Denzin, is to reduce (if not eliminate) bias in the research. By using triangulation we ensure that we have a comprehensive answer to the question.

You may have noticed that at the fourth tier of the Answer Key, there were always a minimum of three measures. This is because of triangulation.

Denzin offers that as you increase the number of differing measures used to provide insight on a single issue, the definitions move from an abstract thought, to validated concept, and finally to proven reality. Although Denzin may not have been the first to coin the term "triangulation"—he cites Eugene J. Webb as the father of the term—I like his explanation. It matches very closely to how I use the term in the context of a metrics program.

If you take the time to research Denzin's use of triangulation, you'll find that it isn't an exact match to how I use the term for metrics. That is partly due to the nature of the use of our results. While Denzin is giving guidance for sociological research that has the purpose of finding deeper truths within his field and having those truths debated and challenged within the scientific community in journals and experiments—our needs (yours and mine) are much simpler and more practical.

Triangulation of Measures

When I created a metrics program for my organization in 2003, I started with the Product/Service Health quadrant (Effectiveness). Yes, I practiced what I preached.

I knew the quadrant. I knew the possible measures that would fit (or at least a starting point). I also knew how to test the measures for alignment with the Product/Service Health quadrant.

But to ensure we gained a comprehensive picture, I fell upon triangulation— the use of three or more measures to answer the question. In the case of effectiveness, we identified the primary measures—Delivery, Usage, and Customer Satisfaction—from the Answer Key.

Rather than select one or two, I determined that we should use all three, which would provide a fuller picture. Each measure had different characteristics in their sources and methods of collection.

Triangulation of Collection Methods and Sources

Triangulation also requires different collection methods, as follows:

- Delivery is an objective (quantitative) internal measure collected without customer involvement. Most times I was able to use automated collection methods for these measures (like trouble call tracking systems, monitoring systems, or time accounting systems). These do not measure customers, but how well the organization delivers the products and services.

- Usage is an objective (quantitative) external measure based on customer behaviors. What do they buy? Who do they call? How often do they use our services? How did they find out about our services and products? How many one-time customers do we have vs. how many repeat customers?

- Customer Satisfaction is a subjective (qualitative) external measure and the most customer-centric of the group. Here, we directly ask the customer for their opinion. A better title for this item would be "customer direct feedback." You ask the customer what they thought of the service and product, but you also ask for ideas for improvement. These questions can be asked in a survey, through focus groups, or through individual interviews. There are pros and cons to each, from varying costs to differing volumes of data collected. You should pick the methods that work best for you. Many times the customer base will dictate the best feedback tools.

You can use other groupings for triangulation. I offer these because I know they work, and they are simple to implement. The idea is to address at least three different viewpoints, sources, and methods of collection.

The concept of triangulation can be used at each level of the metric. I don't suggest you go too deeply or you may find that you are collecting thousands of different measures. I want you to use triangulation at the top level—in the case of effectiveness metrics, at the Delivery, Usage, and Customer Satisfaction level. But, you can use the same concept at the next level down.

For Customer Satisfaction, you could use the following three different methods of collection: surveys, focus groups, and interviews. This can be very expensive, especially interviews. But you could also use two different surveys—the annual survey given to a large portion of your customer base, and the trouble call survey.

You get the idea.

Another example is Delivery. We actually broke Delivery out into three major factors:

- Availability
- Speed
- Accuracy

Each of these were looked at for possible triangulation. Did we have three good ways to measure Availability? How about Speed? Yes. Speed to deliver, speed to resolve, speed to respond for example.

One last way to look at triangulation is through perspectives. We've actually already included this in our three areas of measure. Remember? Delivery was an internal perspective. Usage and Customer Satisfaction were external. There are only two choices here, but when we add in the subjective and objective qualifiers we have a total of four possible choices.

We used only three—external objective, external subjective, and internal objective. Since that early program in 2003, I have since chosen to add a fourth measure area to the Effectiveness quadrant. You may have noticed that we are missing an internal subjective measure. We had the other three permutations, but we never thought to ask the service providers what they thought of the service they were providing.

Remember, you don't have to stop at three. You should use as many different measures, collection methods, sources, and perspectives as necessary to tell the complete story.

Conflicting Results

Because we use varying methods and data sources, we run the real risk of obtaining conflicting results. But, rather than see this as a negative, you should see it as a positive.

Let's look at a restaurant example. If our restaurant's effectiveness metric is made up of Delivery, Usage, and Customer Satisfaction, we may expect that the results of each of these measurement areas should always coincide. If we have good service (Delivery) we should have high Customer Satisfaction ratings. And if we have high Customer Satisfaction, we could assume that we should have high levels of repeat customers, and high usage. We also expect the opposite. If we have poor Customer Satisfaction, we expect that customers won't come back. If we don't deliver well (too slow, wrong items delivered, or the menu items are unavailable) we would expect poor ratings and less usage.

These are logical assumptions, but many times incorrect ones. Each of the permutations tells us something different. In Table 5-1, let's look at each measure with a simple high vs. low result. Of course, the real results of your measures may be much more complicated—especially when you remember that each can also utilize triangulation. Delivery could have high availability and speed to deliver, but poor accuracy. You could have high usage for one type of clientele and low for another. Customer satisfaction could have high marks for some areas (courtesy of staff) and low for others (efficiency of staff). Rather than complicate it further, let's look at the measures at the higher level, keeping in mind the complexity possible when taking into account lower levels of triangulation.

Table 5-1. Interpreting Measures: An Example

Delivery	Usage	Customer Satisfaction	Possible Interpretation
High	High	High	Generally, life should be good. There are other factors to investigate—other metrics to create. It may be time to look at other quadrants in the tier like: Employee Satisfaction and Turnover. Of course, the owner may want to measure how well the business is doing counting the bottom line—is it making money? Future Health would be another area to investigate.
High	Low	High	In this scenario, the issue of low usage is likely due to something other than delivery or customer satisfaction. It could be you have too high of a price point. Your business could be in a poor location. You could suffer from inadequate marketing and advertising.
High	High	Low	You may be the "only game in town." The customer may perceive that you are the only choice for the service/product you offer. Your assessment of your delivery may be correct or out of touch with the customer. If your assessment is correct, then you may be offering a product/service that your customers "need" but not necessarily want. Like flu shots.
High	Low	Low	This case could describe a situation where your menu doesn't fit your clientele. Perhaps your menu is misplaced in the primary neighborhood your restaurant is in. Your pricing could be too high for your customer base.

(*continued*)

Table 5-1. (*continued*)

Delivery	Usage	Customer Satisfaction	Possible Interpretation
Low	High	High	You may be the only source for a niche market. If there is no competition for your product/service, you may likely receive good marks from customer satisfaction. Once again, you may have a monopoly-like situation. When AT&T was Ma Bell, and you only had one choice, customer satisfaction may have been higher, even if customer service wasn't the best. Most times, customer satisfaction isn't an objective observation—it is based on your expectations. If the customer doesn't expect a lot, even mediocre service may rate high.
Low	High	Low	It is even more likely that you have the "only game in town." This could be based on price point (the cheapest food in town), or based on your product or service. If after the largest snow to hit your area stops—you may be very willing to pay the only snow removal service regardless of the quality, speed, or level of customer service.
Low	Low	High	This could be representative of an excellent staff. If you have the nicest wait staff but lousy food, you could see this mix of rating. It could be the customer likes you personally and doesn't want to hurt your feelings, but is unwilling to continue to spend money in your establishment. But it could also be that your delivery expectations are too stringent and you're in a lousy location.

Besides the interpretation of each of the individual measurement areas, the triangulation itself offers information you would lack if you only collected one or two areas.

Using our restaurant business as an example, let's interpret some possible measures. In Table 5-1, you can see how different permutations of the results of the measures can tell a different story. While each measure provides some basic insights, it is more meaningful to look at them in relation to each other.

You may argue that triangulation seems to make the results more confusing, not clearer. But in actuality, triangulation assures that you have more data and more views of that data. The more information you have the better your answers will be. But in all cases the next step should be the same. Investigate, investigate, investigate. The beauty of triangulation is that you already have so many inputs that your investigation can be much more focused and reap greater benefits with less additional work.

Imagine if all you measured was Customer Satisfaction. If you ratings in this area were high, what could you determine? You could think life was good. But if you're not making enough money to keep your business open, you'll wonder what happened.

Triangulation not only allows you to use disparate data to answer a single question, it actually encourages you to do so.

Recap

The Answer Key can help you check the quality of your work and ensure that you're on the right track. And if or when you get stumped and you don't know which direction to go, it can help you get on track.

Most metrics you design, if they fall on the Answer Key, will most likely start at the third tier and belong to one of the following four viewpoints:

- The customers' viewpoint (effectiveness)
- The business's viewpoint (efficiency)
- The workers' viewpoint
- The leadership's viewpoint

As you move from left to right on the Answer Key, you move from the strategic to the tactical. Another way to look at this is that you move from the root question toward data.

Regardless of where your metric (or root question) falls, you'll have to move to the right to find the measures and data you need to answer the question. At the fourth tier we found the following:

- Return vs. Investment
  - Product/Service Health—Customer View
  - Process Health—Business View
- State of the Union
  - Organizational Health—Employee View
  - Future Health—Leadership View

The fourth tier is the most frequently used by my clients. It is far enough left that root questions starting here are worthy of metrics to answer, and far enough right that they are easy for most organizations to comprehend their use in improving the organization.

In the fifth (and any consecutive) tier, we find mostly information and measures. If we find our root question residing here, the question is probably very tactical and may not require a full-blown metric to answer. Remembering the Metric Development Plan, you should flesh out the metric by identifying not only the information and measures, but also document the individual data points needed.

Triangulation is a principal foundation for a strong metric program. Triangulation has many benefits. The more triangulation used, the stronger the benefits. But the saying "all things in moderation" is also true with triangulation. You can overdo anything. You'll need to find the happy medium for you. Let's look at some of the following benefits:

- Higher levels of confidence in the accuracy of the measures used to form the metric

- Higher levels of confidence in the methods used to collect, analyze, and report the measures

- A broader perspective of the answer—increasing the likelihood of an accurate interpretation of the metric

- Satisfaction in knowing that you are "hearing the voice of all your customers"

- A more robust metric (if you lose a measure, data source, or analysis tool, you will have other measures to fall back on)

- Confidence that you are "seeing" the big picture as well as you can

It is important to use triangulation in more than one aspect of the measurement collection and analysis, including the following:

- Multiple sources of data

- Multiple collection methods

- Multiple analysis methods (across measures and the willingness to apply different analytics to the same measures)

- Multiple areas (like Delivery, Usage, and Customer Satisfaction) or categories

With all of this diversity, it is important to stay focused. Collecting data from different quadrants in the Answer Key would not fit the principle of triangulation. If you dilute your answers by mixing the core viewpoint, you will run the risk of becoming lost in the data. If you lose focus and collect data from disparate parts of the Answer Key, it is probable that you are trying to answer multiple questions with only one answer. While meta-metrics use other metrics as part of their input, they must still stay within the context defined by the root question.

A solid metric can lead you in time to metrics in other areas of the Answer Key, but only after you've done your due diligence in answering the questions at hand.

Establishing Standards and Benchmarks

Standards and benchmarks, in the realm of metrics, are strongly interconnected. Standards, from the Industrial Age through today, are invaluable for providing a means for interoperability. Standards in the industrial world allow you to use a light bulb that you bought at Walmart in a lamp that you bought at a high-end designer furniture store. Standards allow you to get gas for your car from any station in the United States, without worrying if the gas pump nozzle will fit into your gas tank. From the ingredients label on a can of soup to the technology that allows you to tune your radio, standards give consistency and interoperability for manufacturers, distributors, builders, and customers alike.

Unlike the manufacturing industry, performance measures are more akin to an art than a science. The use of standards for how we measure things for improvement is arguable. What need is there? If our questions are unique, and thus our answers are unique, why do we need standards for our measures?

Since I advocate creating measures to answer your specific questions, I have trouble taking up the other side of the debate. Why indeed?

I would love to have standards for how you develop metrics; as in the use of expectations over targets, for example. Or for the definition of the data owner. But, standards for performance measures as a whole? Why?

Before I answer this question, let's look at benchmarks and why I think the two are interrelated.

Benchmarks: Best Used to Provide Meaningful Comparisons

Benchmarks are best used to provide meaningful comparisons for your metrics. Outside of defining expectations, you usually want to know how well you perform against your peers. If you're ambitious, you'll want to know how well you perform compared to the best—the best in your industry, the best in your country and, perhaps if you're really ambitious, the best in the world.

Benchmarks are a blessing and a curse.

Benchmarks are also useful for drawing a "line in the sand." You can establish a baseline from your own measures so that you can compare your present performance to your past performance. This is critical when your goal is to improve.

Establish Baselines

One of my joys when working with clients on metrics is helping them establish a baseline; mostly because it forces them to put the metrics upfront in their improvement-process thinking. I almost always run into goals to improve effectiveness, improve efficiency, improve productivity, or improve customer satisfaction.

"Improve" is a lousy verb to use in a goal statement. You have to qualify it with more information—as in "how much" of an improvement? By a certain percentage? By a certain number?

My favorite recollection of the poor use of an "improve" goal was in my parish council. I was hoping to bring organizational development expertise to the council. I was teamed with a retired police officer, a successful business owner, a nurse, our priest, and a retired grandmother. The goal? Improve membership in the church. I wasn't perturbed because I had seen this type of goal (increase, decrease, etc.) many times before.

I said, "Improve membership—by how much?"

"What do you mean?" asked the ex-police officer.

"I mean, if it's our goal to improve membership, how will we know that we achieved it?"

The business owner said, "Oh, you're trying to get us to set a goal."

I countered, "I thought that was the intention—to come up with goals for the year?"

"Yes," said the business owner, "but you're trying to set us up for failure. We'll set a number and if we don't reach it, we will have failed."

Now I sat in stunned silence. I may have actually opened and closed my mouth once or twice. "Uh. Well. Would you be happy with just one more family joining?"

"Sure," said the nurse.

"Anything more than that is gravy!" said the ex-police officer.

I turned to the priest, still in shock. "You'll feel we've achieved this goal if we add just one family?"

He shook his head no. As the leader of the team, and our parish, his input carried the equivalent weight of a CEO.

"How many families join each year now?" I asked

"Two or three a year," the priest answered.

"So if we do nothing, we'd achieve this goal?"

He nodded in the affirmative.

We eventually worked out a reasonable and measurable increase over the expected growth without making any changes. The purpose of the goal was to build up the parish. The purpose of the metric was to see if our efforts were successful. We had plans, ideas, and activities scheduled for the purpose of bringing in new members and bringing back parishioners who had fallen away. We needed to (1) set a goal to focus our efforts and ideas; and (2) set measures to tell us what worked and what didn't.

We also needed a benchmark. We could not determine if any of our efforts were producing the desired result if we didn't know the norm. Consider the benchmark in this case a "control group" or value. You have to know what you get if you do nothing different. Then, when you do new things in new ways, you can at least assume that any changes that you made caused the change to the outcome. Even if you implement so many changes that you can't determine what exactly worked or what exactly didn't work, you at least know whether the overall effort(s) worked.

So, benchmarks basically allow you to know where you are and, therefore, where you end up.

A benchmark is the starting line.

Even when a benchmark is used to compare you against your peers, it is essentially a starting line—a baseline to measure your progress against. The purest form of the benchmark is when you set it as an internal baseline that allows you to measure progress.

Set Benchmarks Responsibly

Benchmarks falter from time to time when leaders want to use the comparison benchmark as the baseline. Most times, it starts with something like, "Can you get our competitors' average availability, response time, or customer satisfaction ratings so that we can compare ourselves to it?"

This requires that the performance of your competitors is a good starting point.

My simple and first argument against chasing this data is: "What if you are already better than your competitors? Does that mean you're doing well enough?"

So, while gathering information on another organization's performance can be enlightening, if your goal is to improve, it is not overly useful. If your goal is to be better than your peers, then, of course, this benchmark is essential. But even if your goal is to be better than your competitors, you'll need to know (1) whether your efforts are helping you improve; and (2) how far you are from the performance of your peers.

If you choose to look only internally at your performance, standards are not necessary. But, if (and when—because eventually you'll want to see how you compare to others) you decide to compare your performance to your peers or competitors, standards will be critical. You can't compare yourself to others when the methods of measurement are different.

Let's say you define the availability of the network as the amount of time without an outage divided by the total amount of time in a given period.

- Availability = 1,440 minutes (number of minutes in one day (or 24 hours)) − 20 minutes (of outage) divided by 1,440 minutes

- Availability = (1,440 − 20) ÷ 1,440 = 98.6%

So far, so good. But, let's say your closest competitor (or peer) has a 100 percent availability rate for the same period. Are you going to step up your game a bit? Are you going to work harder? Is your competitor doing better than you?

Well, without standards, you can't tell if your competitor is doing a better job than you. What if you define an outage as any time span that your customers cannot use the network, but your competitors consider an outage as only those times when the network is unavailable due to unscheduled or unplanned downtime? In other words, let's say that during the same 24-hour period, your competitor had scheduled maintenance for four hours. If you define an outage as any time the service is unavailable (which is likely the way customers will interpret it), then the competitor's availability *should* be reported as follows:

- Competitor Availability: $(1,440 - 240) \div 1,440 = 83.3\%$

If you had all of the raw data for your competitor's reports, you could use your personal "standard" and determine how well you perform against your competitor. But this is highly unlikely to happen. What you will get, if you are extremely lucky, is the "score".

So, how you define an outage compared to the way your competitor defines an outage is critical to your use of their measures as a benchmark.

Standards Allow Comparison to Others

Standards in performance measurement come down to providing the ability to compare measures between different organizations. Just as manufacturing standards allow you to use your products seamlessly with another organization's products, standards in performance measurement allow you to "use your measures" seamlessly with another organization's measures. If there were standardization of performance measures, you could "borrow" another unit's measures for your own purposes. If you had the same questions, you could trust that that metrics used by Company A could be used to measure the same things in your organization.

Without standards, it is hard to imagine how you could use the metrics of a different organization—even if you had the same exact root questions. And using measures produced by another organization as a benchmark is even more improbable.

Getting Good Data

This problem with benchmarks and standards for performance measurement also creates problems for well-meaning organizations that seek to provide data warehouses of information. This information invariably is intended for your comparison. To make the data warehouse effective, it has to have a clear set of standards for the information provided by the different organizations.

HDI, a third-party survey company, offers benchmarking on customer satisfaction data by controlling data definitions. HDI administers the survey to your customers, collects the responses, and provides you with reports, analysis, and raw data. Since HDI standardizes its questions (the same questions are asked along with the same set of possible replies on a 5-point Likert scale), it is able to offer you comparisons against other organizations, including the following:

- Comparison of your scores (average, percentage satisfied, or other) against all other organizations who have used the HDI service

- Comparison of your scores with others in your industry (self-selected from a list)

- Comparison of your scores to the top nth percentile of others' customer base

This provides you with a higher confidence in the comparability of the information. Of course, there are some drawbacks. Only organizations that use HDI's service are included in the comparison, and your main competitors or peers may not be among these organizations. Even if you compare your results against the entire customer base, this still may not reflect the pool you want to compare to. Another minor drawback is that you are forced to use one set of questions. No deviations. If you want to use the 10-point scale suggested by Reichheld in *The Ultimate Question*, you could not use HDI's service. And even if you could use the 10-point scale, you could not compare the data to those who used a 5-point scale.

The Goal: Reliable Industry Standards

Industry standards for performance measures would make it possible to truly benchmark, rank, and compare peer organizations. It should be feasible to convince an *industry* (like higher education IT) to standardize performance measures before the chance of adopting *universal* standards. The tighter you can make the pool for standardization, the easier it should be to come to agreement. Higher education information technology is a pretty specific pool. If you started with information technology performance measures—your pool for coming to consensus on the standards is too large. If you narrow it to *education* information technology, you're doing better. *Higher education* tightens it a little more.

Consensus is required for success. Publishing a standard does not make it effective. You must have the majority of organizations (in your industry) using the standard to make it useful. Since you need high participation in the use of the standards, it logically follows that you should involve as many of the target audience in the creation of the standard as possible

I offer that the consortium structure is the best bet for creating standards for performance measures. The consortium creates, evaluates, reviews, and manages standards for an industry. The problem may be that the "industry" in this case is hard to define. Of course, if you do as I suggested and find a tighter definition of the target audience, you can make it happen. But, looking at performance measurement as an industry is obviously too large. So, as a performance measurement expert, you'll have to define your "industry" to build a consortium. If you have some standards for performance measurement to reference, you are ahead of the game.

Recap

Standards are tools that allow for interoperability. In the case of performance measures, standards allow for comparison between organizations.

Benchmarks are either the starting line (baseline) for your improvement efforts or a goal for you to achieve. As a baseline, it helps you determine how far you have to progress to achieve your goals, how well you're getting there, and how far you have come. As a goal, it represents how good you want to become—"as good as Company A" or "better than the average."

To have real external benchmarks, you must have standards that are in agreement among the organizations you choose to compare to.

If you can find or develop standards for your performance measures, and your peers agree to them, you can compare measures.

Tools and Resources

Tools can be (and often are) confused with resources. I'll use a simple delineation between the two. Tools are items that can be used to *do*—to actually design, create, analyze, and publish metrics. An example is Microsoft Excel.

On the other hand, resources provide information that provides guidance or knowledge used for designing, creating, analyzing, and publishing metrics. Rather than an analysis tool (like Minitab), resources include textbooks on how to use software or perform statistical analysis, how-to videos, articles, blogs, books, and discussion groups (such as those found on networking sites like LinkedIn). There are also organizations (new and established) that you can join and participate in to learn more about metrics.

In this appendix, I'll share some of my favorite tools and some that come highly recommended by colleagues and friends. Please don't buy any of these tools on the basis of their inclusion here; instead, if something sounds good to you, research it further. Just as with metrics themselves—you'll need to marry the possibilities to your specific requirements. Based on your root questions, your environment, and the programs you develop—different tools and resources may be called for.

Tools

Some tools play multiple roles, but most specialize in a primary function and have other functions as a supplement. Most trouble-ticket tracking tools work this way. They are designed (and do a good job at) capturing and tracking trouble tickets, and may also provide basic graphing tools. They don't provide much in analysis; and provide nothing toward being a complete metric tool. But trouble-tracking tools are good at what they are supposed to do. The key is not to try to make a specific tool do more than it is designed to do.

The really good news is that a meaningful and useful metrics program doesn't require a ton of statistical analysis or complicated charting. Always keep in mind that the purpose of a metrics program is to provide insights that can support decisions, direct investigations, and expose areas of concern.

Tools simply provide different ways of looking at the information you've gathered. Depending on your root question and what you are trying to learn from your metric, you can use many different forms of analysis. The tools I cover in this appendix are the few that I find useful and simple. They are simple for me to produce/use and simple for my audience to understand. Always remember your audience when displaying your metrics. Even if you use more complex analysis to get to your answers, you may need to find ways to display them in more simplistic terms.

Microsoft Excel

I've found Excel to be much more than spreadsheet software. I guess it was originally created to assist with accounting or bookkeeping. Ages ago, I used to explain that spreadsheet programs were good for working on numbers. If you wanted to perform math on your data, spreadsheets were the way to go. Today, Microsoft Excel has grown to be much more than a glorified calculator. I use it for much of my metrics work. Like most current software applications, Excel has more capabilities than most users realize or will ever use. Besides the breadth of functionality, Excel also provides a lot of flexible power, as in macros (mini programs), PowerPivot, and PowerView. I collect, analyze, and produce graphs for most of my work in Excel. With Excel add-ins, I can also perform more complex analysis inside the spreadsheets. With Excel 2013, I can handle as many records as I need. I use Excel as the foundation for my work.

Excel has a statistical add-in that comes with the full version, but you have to "turn it on." It doesn't come with this functionality preset. Turning it on will give you some basic statistical tools like histograms and regression tests.

SigmaXL

SigmaXL is a tool that can be accessed through Excel. It creates a more intuitive set of menu items in its own tab than the statistical add-in that comes with Excel. I was especially happy to find that it had a BoxPlot tool (graph), which I was unable to find in any other add-in. I am truly impressed with the SigmaXL capabilities.

Minitab

While working on my Green Belt in Six Sigma, I fell in love with SigmaXL. Before the honeymoon was over, my instructors told me about Minitab. They described it as better, smarter, easier to use, and more comprehensive than SigmaXL. The biggest problem with statistics is they're just too hard to deal with, especially for the benefits gained. SigmaXL makes it worth the effort; and *if* Minitab is better (I haven't used it yet), I want a copy.

Visualization Tools

Visualization tools are primarily (if not solely) designed to provide access to your data—in the form of dashboards, scorecards, or other visualizations. These can be used for metrics per my definition.

Theoris Vision Software

Theoris Vision Software provides a dashboard and reporting solution that includes charts, graphs, scorecards, maps, and ad-hoc reports. Everything is driven from the dashboards. I like that I can create my own visual and reporting content pretty easily. From what I've seen, the real power of this application lies in the unique ability it has to map to various data sources and files, instead of the traditional approach of pulling everything together into a spreadsheet or database.

Vision is not a metric design tool per se, but it is a powerful tool for visualizing your measures. It also allows others (stakeholders) to access your metrics on their own. I especially like the ability to set up hierarchies in the data, which in turn allows viewers to drill down into their data further. This capability is further expanded to allow the creation of ad-hoc reports at different levels of information. This can be a bad thing—depending on the level of maturity of your audience—but for the most part, it's pretty slick. Overall, this is really an impressive tool for displaying metrics and starting those critical conversations. Currently, Vision is mostly focused on the health industry, but the competition had better watch out as Vision branches into other industries. A really nice tool which I've added to my wish list.

iDashboards

iDashboards is exactly what you'd imagine by its name: an excellent tool for creating and displaying dashboards—or compilations of Key Process Indicators (what I'd call measures). With iDashboards, you could use your measures to create a view of your metric for a given question.

I like both Vision and iDashboards for this purpose. The question for me then becomes cost and ease of use. If you are thinking of obtaining a tool for displaying your data in this manner, I'd encourage you to spend time demo-ing both products. This one is also on my wish list—and I'll be happy with either as a surprise for Christmas.

Tableau

Tableau is not an add-in, but it works well with Excel. You can easily import data into Tableau from Excel or other common tools. Tableau's power is in the ability to quickly and easily try different graphical representations (visualizations) of your data. I know some people who love it and use it before they do any thorough analysis. I haven't found it works for me, but I do see the potential value (I have a copy, but haven't been able to put it to a lot of use).

Survey Tools

The following three survey tools each offer different benefits. In order, the first provides some useful analysis of what's important to your customers as well as how well you provide those services. The second is a third-party service (not really a tool in the true sense) and makes the survey work easy. The last is a favorite of mine as it allows you to create what you need, customizing your surveys to fit your requirements (and the cost is attractive).

TechQual+

TechQual+ (www.techqual.org) is a good example of a survey tool; it was created by my friend Timothy Chester, the CIO at the University of Georgia. Most of the questions are preset in TechQual+, causing some limitations; but these are also its strengths. Since the questions are standardized, you can compare your results to others who chose to use this tool. There are other third-party survey organizations (HDI, for example), but a large benefit of TechQual+ is that it is free.

HDI

The HDI Customer Satisfaction Index is a survey service. HDI does everything for you: they survey your customers, tabulate your results, and provide you with reports in multiple formats. They also provide comparisons to others (for example, by industry or all other customers). HDI is only one example; there are other third-party survey services that offer this service. I suggest you price shop *and* look for ones that already have a large customer base in *your* industry. Customer satisfaction surveying is an interesting business niche.

SurveyMonkey

I confess—I like SurveyMonkey; partly because it's free (if you use it sparingly; though, if you want to use it on a larger scale, the costs are very reasonable), but mostly because of its simplicity. With SurveyMonkey, you build the survey; then you provide a link to the survey to your customers. SurveyMonkey also offers simple analysis tools, but I usually download the results into Excel and do my own analysis.

IT Solutions/Business Intelligence Tools

Many "IT solution" companies now include dashboards and scorecards in their service packages. This is a clear indicator of the need for metrics and the power of software to help deliver them. IT solutions packages may include the metrics tools as an add-in to the suite of services—pulling the data byproducts from key offerings (process control, management, architectural design, etc.).

The major difference I've found between these tools and the stand-alone tools is in the scope. If you don't need (or can't afford) a large-scale solution set, you can get a lot out of the tools specifically designed for metrics. If you're looking at purchasing (or already own) a large-scale IT solution, you may want to look into its capabilities to also provide metrics assistance.

ASE 10

An example of a data-centric toolset for organizational improvement using scorecards, dashboards, and measurements is ASE 10, from ActiveStrategy (activestrategy.com). It's a bit complex, but offers pricing based on company size. ASE 10 is heavily based on predefined methodologies, but seems to have enough flexibility to work with the metrics that you design. I haven't used this tool, but it has been recommended by a colleague whose opinion I trust.

The issue for most larger-scale tools is that they may offer too much. Ignoring the cost, these tools offer more capability than most people need—especially if you are just starting on your metrics journey.

Other Tools

Other tools may not fit the definition of a metric tool at all, but be very helpful to your metric efforts. The two examples I offer are at different ends of a scope/size spectrum. QPR is a larger scale process improvement tool which has useful applications to a metrics effort. PowerPivot is a tool which works with (and "in") Excel.

QPR

QPR (QPR.com) is an example of a business-driven solution. Its scope is so large that I can't tell you about it all. QPR is used mostly by companies outside of the United States; but I believe it will make a big splash on our shores soon. Rather than a simple, lower cost, limited-use tool, QPR's solution is a mid-range, enterprise-level solution.

QPR's web-based solutions can be selected based upon your need. If you need to build an understanding of your processes, one of its tools, "Process Analyzer," assists in developing business process diagrams using a logging file input structure. If you need to share your database of business processes, "ProcessDesigner" provides that solution. Most metric-centered reporting requirements can be satisfied with the "Metrics" solution. If you need to integrate business process reporting and metrics, a combination of these solutions provide you with an integrated management reporting system.

The cost will reflect its expansive power. I include it as an example of a high-end tool, and because it does so much more (process analysis, process management, etc.) than metrics, the higher costs are no surprise. I especially like that such a nice enterprise-level solution includes specific tools for metrics.

PowerPivot

Unlike most of the tools, PowerPivot isn't an analytical tool at all. It allows you to use Excel to be more like its brother, Microsoft Access—a database tool. Although most metrics are number-based efforts, there are many times when it would be useful to have a relational view of the data. A relational database would be the perfect tool *if* it had the ability to do mathematical and statistical analysis on the data. PowerPivot promises to give you the best of both worlds—a number-based program you can treat as a relational database.

Resources

Whereas I told you to research before you buy any tools (tools are high-cost compared to a book or a membership in an organization), in this section, I recommend you try the resource. If you don't want to buy the book, check it out from your local library. For the most part, to determine the usefulness of a resource, you'll need to have complete access. Most of the resources I offer are either free or low-cost (less than $50).

When you search for resources, depending on your industry, you will find many to choose from. In the information technology arena, I've been hearing a lot about the COBIT framework, ISO/IEC 20000 (international standard for IT service management), and the Information Technology Infrastructure Library (ITIL).

Rather than provide you a list of web sites, I will share some ways to perform a search. Search engines offer results in different formats: video, web, images, blogs, shopping, etc. Most useful will be web, video, and blogs. The web classification is where you'll find everything from articles in e-zines, books, and encyclopedic definitions, to how-to guides for developing metrics.

If you search "metrics" you will find too many results on the metric system of measurement. You'll want to narrow your search. "Performance Metrics" will bring you a lot closer to what you're looking for. Even then, you may want to narrow your search depending on your particular needs and industry. For example, you can search on "IT metrics" or "IT performance metrics" if you are in the information technology arena. You can also search on "business intelligence" (the newest catch phrase for data-based decision making) or "IT solutions."

Depending on your industry, you may find a healthy store of standards, benchmarks, and predefined data, measures, and information for your metrics. The financial industry is one example of a robust metric environment. Another is the manufacturing industry. If you are reading this book, you are not likely in an industry that has an established metrics framework. Chances are you are in need of meaningful metrics for your organization and your processes. Even so, you can learn from other industries and their metrics. You may be able to leverage some existing works for your own metrics efforts.

A simple search via your favorite web-based search engine returns a long list of measurement, statistical analysis, and metrics tools. I won't provide you with a list that you can visit on your own. Instead I offer insights and a short list of resources and references.

While I built the list from tools and references that I've personally used, I highly recommend that you do what I've preached from the beginning—investigate for yourself. I have found some books to be "on target" and others to have views that I would argue strongly against. Every book, blog, and article I've read has been useful in developing my overall view and concepts about metrics. Even the ones I've found outlandishly off-target have proven to be beneficial to the overall concept I offer in this book.

Don't discard the entire work because you find some portions to be "wrong," in your viewpoint. You can learn much from those who disagree with you. One of my colleagues who helped in the writing of this book disagreed with me more often than we agreed; it was one of the reasons that I asked him to be the technical reviewer for the book. I trusted him to provide an honest view, even if it were a totally dissenting one. While I believe in the concepts and tools I've presented, I'm open to other opinions. I welcome them as they should help to make my understanding of how to make metrics work better.

I want you to look at the resources and references listed here, and any others you investigate later, in the same way. There are no silver bullets, there is no holy grail. There is no one right way to do organizational development or process improvement. There is no one way to do metrics. Stay open to new ideas and different opinions. And always make sure what you use works for you. Don't use it because I or anyone else say to, use it because you've tried it and it works for you.

So, let's look at some of the resources and references I've found useful in my metric journey.

Web Sites

The following are web sites that I've found useful.

XPC Palladium Group

XPC (http://community.thepalladiumgroup.com) is primarily a community for discussing Balanced Scorecard methods, but I have found it a good place to converse on metrics in general. Most of the participants on the site are disciples of Kaplan and Norton and believe in using measurement in ways I disagree with. The good news is they are open to other opinions. It is a well-run web site. Just recently I have heard that they are going to charge for membership—and as you may have ascertained from my opinions on tools, I don't believe in paying for the opportunity to network. As with all of my recommendations, check it out (especially if you have to pay) before you buy.

LinkedIn

I like networking; especially networking for professionals. In addition to the LISTSERVs I participate in through different organizations, I enjoy LinkedIn (www.linkedin.com). LinkedIn groups allow for conversations and discussions on pretty much any topic you want—and you can simply create a new group/topic if it doesn't exist. I belong to more than one group concerned with metrics (Performance Measurement, IT Performance Measurement, and IT Metrics–CEITPS) and have found them to be very useful. And membership is free.

The Consortium for the Establishment of Information Technology Performance Measures (CEITPS)

CEITPS (www.ceitps.org) is a nonprofit organization that I founded for the sole purpose of developing standards for IT performance measures. It is a very young organization. All standards created by this organization will be made available free to the public via the web site. Membership has a minimal fee and the biggest benefit you get for your money is that you are given the opportunity to help in creating and voting on the standards. The membership income is used to pay for the web presence only.

smartKPIs

smartKPIs.com is a repository of **K**ey **P**rocess **I**ndicators (measures). Since it offers free access to a good portion of its KPIs, I think it is worthy of mention. I can't recommend paying for any of their offerings (only premium subscribers have access to calculation, references, and PDF export and filtering functionalities) as it goes against my beliefs toward benchmarks and canned metrics. But, if you want to see what others have come up with, the free catalog of examples is a good place to start.

I won't repeat all of the cautions I've offered in the book—but I will suggest that if you use this (or other comparable references) that you do so with a grain of salt *and* also ask around. Your industry peers should be great sources, and by asking them you'll build your relationships and your professional network.

Books

These books helped me immensely when I was trying to get my head and arms around metrics. I think they will help you too.

How to Measure Anything

How to Measure Anything: Finding the Value of Intangibles in Business by Douglas W. Hubbard (John Wiley & Sons, 2007). I love Hubbard's positive, can-do attitude when it comes to finding ways to measure literally anything. I especially enjoyed his work on calibrating your ability to estimate accurately. Some of it was a little too deep for me, but I found almost all of it useful and an easy read. All in all, it is a nice text on how to measure and estimate—untethered to any specific improvement methodology. I recommend this book, but suggest you may find yourself picking and choosing chapters to read or reference.

Transforming Performance Measurement

Transforming Performance Measurement: Rethinking the Way We Measure and Drive Organizational Success by Dr. Dean R. Spitzer (American Management Association, 2007) is another favorite. I found it easy to read (with minor exceptions). I consider Dean a kindred spirit. Most of my disagreements come in how to deal with the fear, uncertainty, and doubt that surround metrics.

I find that we are on the same wavelength, however, when it comes to the problems and hurdles you have to overcome to make metrics work. I believe we go to the "same church, different pew." Definitely worth the read.

The Intelligent Company

The Intelligent Company by Bernard Marr (John Wiley & Sons, 2010) is yet another favorite. I came upon it well into the writing of this book and knew that I had found another member of the metrics family. As with Dr. Spitzer's book, I found a fair amount to argue against in Marr's book. But I find this book more useful than one with too much jargon or technical speak. I learn a lot (more) from viewpoints different than my own. Overall there is more that I agree with than I disagree with *and* it's an "easy" read. I recommend this book for your library.

Measuring What Matters

Measuring What Matters: Simplified Tools for Aligning Teams and Their Stakeholders, by Rod Napier & Rich McDaniel (Davies-Black Publishing, 2006). I found this book to be less a guide for developing metrics and more a manual for the American Society for Quality (ASQ). That's not a bad thing, but it wasn't as much help with developing metrics as I would have liked, especially based on the title. I like it much more as a general organizational development book than a metrics book. It's worth a perusal.

Why Organizations Struggle So Hard to Improve So Little

If you're interested in organizational development, I humbly include *Why Organizations Struggle So Hard to Improve So Little: Overcoming Organizational Immaturity*, by Michael Langthorne, Donald Padgett, and me. I've actually read it twice since it was published in 2010 by Greenwood. It is a very easy read with important insights to why you may be struggling to improve or change your organization. The chapter on metrics makes a good introduction to this book. If you're looking at implementing organizational change, I recommend you read it.

Other Books

There are books that I wouldn't recommend for the purpose of developing a metrics program, but are useful in performing analysis; and if you have room on your library shelves, it wouldn't hurt to include them. One that I like in particular is *IT Measurement: Practical Advice from the Experts* (Addison-Wesley, 2002) a compilation by the International Function Point Users Group. I have a special place in my metrics heart for this group since my first metrics mentor, Errol Shim, was a past president of the national group. The 43-chapter book was written by a variety of experts. Some definite gems can be mined here—and hopefully I've given you the tools necessary to find the gems that fit your needs.

Recap

Tools are useful for performing the work—designing, creating, analyzing, and publishing metrics. Resources are references that make doing the work easier or better. Unfortunately, tools can be expensive. The good news is that the methods I've offered for developing a metrics program don't require any particular tools. You can do quite well with whatever tools you have already available. But as you become proficient at metrics development, you may want more out of your toolset, so I offered some tools to consider or explore. Remember, it's only a starting point—find what will work best to meet your requirements and your budget.

Resources, on the other hand, should be investigated as early as possible. I'd be flattered if you only used this book: dog-eared it, highlighted the best passages, wrote in the margins, and used it to help you develop your metrics program. But, chances are you won't agree with everything I've offered. Or you may want confirmation through other works. Or you may feel that I left some gaps in your comprehension of the material. I encourage you to read other books, articles, and papers on the topic.

I have faith in what I've been teaching on metrics and I welcome arguments to the contrary. If the concepts within this book are correct, then they will stand up to thorough scrutiny. To that end, feel free to contact me and offer your opinions—be they in agreement or disagreement. Join me on LinkedIn discussion groups, send me an e-mail, or post your thoughts, questions, or arguments on my web site. The bottom line is simple: do something! Learn more, try more, do more. Share your opinions, try the suggestions I've offered, create a meaningful metric and see how it goes.

Now Comes the Hard Part

The hard part is putting any or all of this into practice.

I consider one of my first mentors in metrics, Erroll Shim, a giant of a man. I consider him a giant in his field, function point analysis and metric analysis. He taught me a great deal and he helped set me on the path that led to the development of much of what you've read here. His expertise was very impressive—he would accurately predict the complexity of a software change and estimated correctly the effort and time required (which were normally very different than our unit had estimated).

But, the problem was that his abilities were his own. They weren't transferrable. It was borne of years of experience. I wanted to develop a simplified method to provide the types of insights he produced independently, to anyone who needed it. These insights were at once more general in nature (they deal with metrics across the business spectrum) and specific in the methodology—building from a root question, using data, measures, information, and other metrics to tell a complete story.

I want you to develop meaningful metrics. I want you to be able to do so without obtaining a certificate in statistics, buying expensive tools, or spending months in training. I believe I've given you the knowledge to make a good start. But you'll need more than a good effort.

Unfortunately, even if you follow the guidance in this book, you will encounter more than a fair share of resistance. It would be nice if you could introduce any of the concepts I've offered—from root questions, to the metrics framework and taxonomy, to the use of documentation, how to use and not use metrics, the Answer Key, triangulation, starting with Effectiveness—without having to fight for their acceptance.

When I attempted to create a metrics program for my own organization, I ran into a lot of resistance. I believed it stemmed from the "no prophet is accepted in his own village" syndrome. But after helping others develop and implement metrics programs, I now believe it's deeper than that. Don't get me wrong, the syndrome does make it difficult. Even if you are an outside consultant, the refrain will be raised—"Just ask the customer! Our customer satisfaction surveys are enough!" Not only will it be shouted, a chorus will rise up in strong harmony.

Even today, I have to fight for a multi-measure metric. Not just using more than two measures, but using ones from different views within the same quadrant.

I don't mean to discourage you. In fact, I hope to do the opposite. I'm hoping that you use the concepts, tools, and techniques in this book to stop chasing data, stop using measures improperly, and to create meaningful metrics for improvement.

I hope that this book has provided you with what you need to plan and design effective metrics and I pray you have the strength of will to follow it.

I

Index

Get the eBook for only $10!

Now you can take the weightless companion with you anywhere, anytime. Your purchase of this book entitles you to 3 electronic versions for only $10.

This Apress title will prove so indispensible that you'll want to carry it with you everywhere, which is why we are offering the eBook in 3 formats for only $10 if you have already purchased the print book.

Convenient and fully searchable, the PDF version enables you to easily find and copy code—or perform examples by quickly toggling between instructions and   applications. The MOBI format is ideal for your Kindle, while the ePUB can be utilized on a variety of mobile devices.

Go to www.apress.com/promo/tendollars to purchase your companion eBook.

Other Apress Business Titles You Will Find Useful

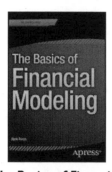

The Basics of Financial Modeling
Avon
978-1-4842-0872-4

Supplier Relationship Management
Schuh/Strohmer/Easton/Hales/Triplat
978-1-4302-6259-6

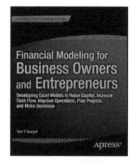

Financial Modeling for Business Owners and Entrepreneurs
Sawyer
978-1-4842-0371-2

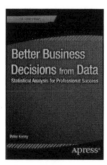

Better Business Decisions from Data
Kenny
978-1-4842-0185-5

Improving Profit
Cleland
978-1-4302-6307-4

Financial Ratios for Executives
Rist/Pizzica
978-1-4842-0732-1

Design Thinking for Entrepreneurs and Small Businesses
Ingle
978-1-4302-6181-0

Plan to Turn Your Company Around in 90 Days
Lack
978-1-4302-4668-8

Common Sense
Tanner
978-1-4302-4152-2

Available at www.apress.com